THE HOME EXPERIENCE

MARILYN WEIHER

...making your home a
Sanctuary of Love
and a Haven of Peace

ᴥ ᴥ ᴥ

THE HOME EXPERIENCE

Published by Living Smart Resources
A division of Kingdom Global Ministries
Copyright © 2006 by Living Smart Resources

Founder of The Mentoring Mansion & The Home Experience: Devi Titus
Authors: Devi Titus and Marilyn Weiher
Design concept by PERSONALITY

FILE CATEGORIES
   Home and Family Life
   Women—Successful Living
   Relationships
   Mentoring Curriculum
   Christian Inspiration

FOR ORDERING
www.mentoringmansion.com

ISBN 978-1-4243-2943-4
Printed in Korea by bigger dot

"By wisdom a house is built, and through understanding it is established; through knowledge its rooms are filled with rare and beautiful treasures."

Proverbs 24:3-4

INTRODUCTION

Research demonstrates that a loving and peaceful home environment affects the well being of an individual socially, emotionally and spiritually. Likewise, when these are absent from the home, insecurity and dysfunction abound. Truly, home is where the heart is formed.

I had the privilege of growing up in a loving and peaceful home. Respect, responsibility and stewardship were woven into the fabric of our family. Although our house was old and plain and sometimes cluttered, it was grand central station for friends and family. When an unexpected guest arrived, we instinctively knew to scoot over a little and add a plate because there was always room for one more person at Mom's table. It made no difference whether you were a traveling evangelist or the town drunk, everyone was welcome and important.

Devi Titus

I have spoken to as many as 20,000 women a year and have come to realize that loving and peaceful homes are becoming extinct. What God intended to be a haven of peace and a sanctuary of love has been reduced to a breeding ground of havoc and despair. Families are stressed because of disrespectful and angry children. Healthy meals are substituted with processed or fast food. Schedules are too busy to include a tidy and clean environment and fatigue has replaced intimacy with our spouses. We know that our families are important yet when it comes to finding a solution to these ever-increasing problems in our lives, we often feel unequipped and overwhelmed.

I believe that my life purpose is to meet the challenge to educate, train and mentor women in how to navigate and implement their very important role in our homes. *The Home Experience* has been dedicated to meeting this objective by applying practical Biblical principles to everyday living. Whether you are a Bible reader or not, you will see how making small intentional choices can result in positive transforming changes. *The Home Experience* is an excellent resource guide in helping to develop a fresh understanding of the importance and impact your home environment can make on your family and friends.

Your home can be loving and peaceful. As you begin walking out *The Home Experience* principles, you will witness restored relationships and find order where there was once chaos. Where you once felt overwhelmed and hopeless, you will be empowered to make a difference. This book has been purposely crafted for your personal pleasure and your spiritual pursuit. You will also learn techniques in sharing this good news with others. The How to Mentor chapter offers creative and easy ideas to use in your home for the training and instruction of these simple principles with the women who you desire to touch their lives.

Marilyn Weiher is that kind of lady in my life. I have been one of several mentors to Marilyn. Her teachable spirit and quest to apply truth reformed her to bring love, peace and order into her home life. My relationship with my husband, the character of my grown children and grandchildren all became role models for her and her young family. Because of years of trusted friendship with Marilyn, her educational and professional background, and her mentoring qualities, I have ask her to participate with me in creating this guide to pass the principles that have transformed our lives on to you so you too can make an impact in your marriage and family life.

My heart's desire for every reader—whether married or single— is that you will be committed to allowing God's love and peace to be a priority in your home. As you unpack these principles for yourself, I ask that you become proactive in sharing the responsibility of mentoring others. Together we can make a difference on the generations to come, one home at a time. The dignity and sanctity of the home will be restored.

Be inspired. Be equipped. Be encouraged. Experience love. Experience peace. It's never too late to improve.

You are awesome,

Devi Titus

Devi Titus 2:3-5

DEVI TITUS & MARILYN WEIHER

Devi Titus is a renowned conference speaker and pastor's wife of over 40 years. She is the founder of VIRTUE magazine and The Mentoring Mansion and now, THE HOME EXPERIENCE— both an inspiring book to read and a mentoring curriculum.

Her innovative approach to ministry continually creates new venues for helping women reach their full potential. She speaks from conviction and motivates with passion. Her personality is infectious. Author Bunny Wilson says of Devi, "When you meet her, you experience her!"

Marilyn Weiher has been part of The Mentoring Mansion team as Devi's teaching partner since its inception. She has experienced transformation in her personal life and marriage because of the impacting principles defined in this book. Marilyn is a professional educator and holds a Master's Degree in Counseling.

Grateful Expressions from Devi

❧ **...to Larry Titus—my wonderful loving husband.** Larry has demonstrated to me a level of love that continually keeps me climbing. He is my drum-major—the rhythm and balance in my life. He believes in me like no one else and always encourages me to pursue my passions. His love and peace stabilized our family.

❧ **...to my Mother—a river of wise instruction.** Mom and Dad's practical pursuit of godliness demonstrated to me real power in the face of religion, which I wanted nothing of. Mom maintained an environment of hospitality, love, and peace in our home while working full time. I experienced with my mother and father the principles that I now teach.

❧ **...to my children, Trina Titus Lozano and Dr. Aaron P. Titus—my heart's delight.** Trina and Aaron's families have made personal choices in their lives to continue our generational rich family heritage—to cherish a godly home and keep the family together at all costs. They are training our grandchildren in godly character and they both constantly serve others with hospitality in their homes—a true family value.

❧ **...Marilyn Weiher—an incredible lady and a faithful friend.** She is a true partner in this venture. When I developed the Mentoring Mansion concept, I asked Marilyn to be a principle instructor. The topics in my syllabus were divided between us. For this reason, Marilyn has written a portion of this material and without her commitment, this book would not exist. She is a wonderful friend and an excellent educator. She lives what she teaches.

❧ **...to the Mentoring Mansion teams.** Teams of volunteer women have served at the various Mentoring Mansion locations, making it possible to host four-day Home Mentoring Intensives. They faithfully prepare the home with excellence, magnificently present meals and maintain peace while each guest is being radically transformed. You are vital to the mission of restoring the dignity and sanctity of the home and I thank you with all my heart.

❧ **...to the thousands of women in audiences who listen to me.** Without you, I would have no reason to rise in the mornings. I am blessed by your eagerness to be all you can be. You come, you listen, and you purchase necessary products to continue to listen to me when you go home. I am grateful that maybe, just maybe, something that I say will elevate your standard of living. I believe in you and know that you will love others in the same way God loves you. I know that you can create and maintain peace and love in your home and family life.

❧ **...to you who have chosen to read this book.** You may be passionate to learn. You may be desperate. You may be curious. Regardless of the reason you have chosen this book, I believe that something you read will unlock your heart and fully release your woman-power to make life-impacting contributions to your family. Don't be afraid. Embrace every truth with an open spirit and enjoy your new journey. Oh yes, be sure to pass on to others everything good that you know because—you can do it!

Grateful Expressions from Marilyn

❧ **...to Devi, my mentor and friend I am eternally thankful for all that you have taught me.** Thank you for inviting me into your life. Your love, patience, instruction, and at times correction have helped shape my life and family values. I am extremely honored and humbled to be a part of this endeavor with you. I treasure your friendship, generosity, and all the opportunities you have opened up for me.

❧ **...to Mike, my fabulous husband and best friend.** Thank you for your support and leadership. Without your encouragement, editing expertise, and fine example I could not have completed this project. I've learned so much from you. Your love has lifted me.

❧ **...to my beautiful daughters, Ellie and Sarah, the joy of my life.** Thank you for all that you've deposited into our home experience. Your lives demonstrate that these principles work. Thank you for your contributions at home to serve your Dad and me while I've worked on this project.

Sanctuary of Love

ESSENTIAL PRINCIPLES

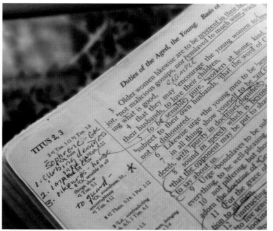

VITAL RELATIONSHIP SKILLS

Haven of Peace

A Mentor's Guide

P.S.

Sanctuary

ESSENTIAL PRINCIPLES

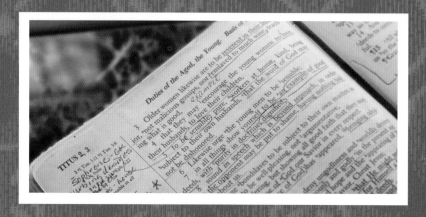

y of Love

VITAL RELATIONSHIP SKILLS

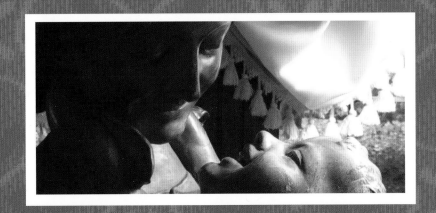

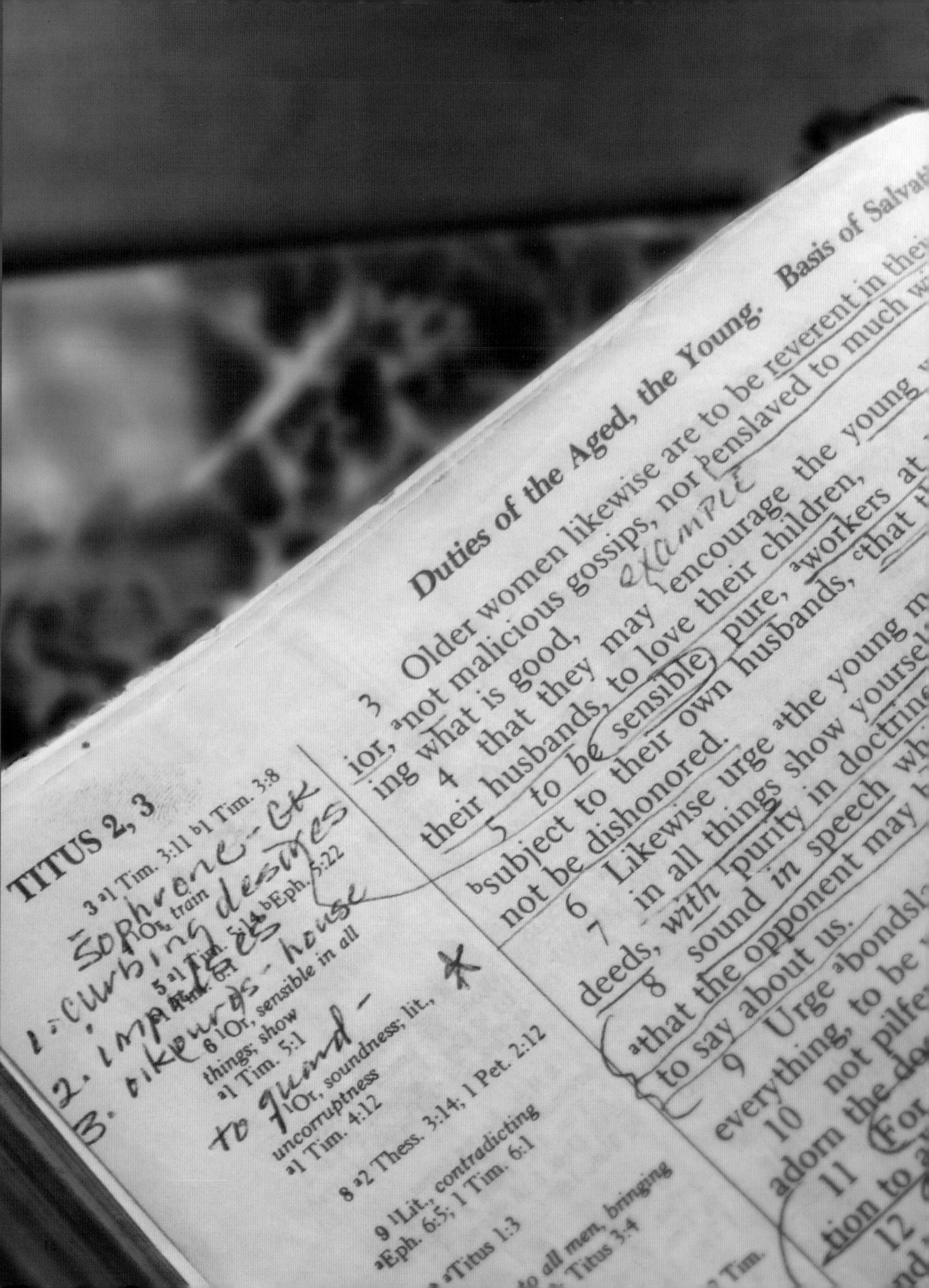

3 Older women likewise are to be reverent in their
ior, ᵃnot malicious gossips, nor ᵇenslaved to much w
ing what is good,

4 that they may ᵃencourage the young w
their husbands, to love their children,

5 to be sensible, pure, ᵃworkers at
ᵇsubject to their own husbands, ᶜthat t
not be dishonored.

6 Likewise urge ᵃthe young m

7 in all things show yoursel
deeds, with ᵃpurity in doctrine
sound in speech wh

8 ᵃthat the opponent may
to say about us.

9 Urge ᵃbondsla
everything, to be

10 not pilfe
adorn the do

11 For
tion to a

12

Handwritten margin notes:

sophrone – GK
1. curbing desires
   ⁵ ¹Or, train
2. impure⁵ ⁴ᵇEph. 5:22
   ⁵ ¹Tim. 2:15
3. oikourgos – house-

3 ᵃ1 Tim. 3:11 ᵇ1 Tim. 3:8

⁶ ¹Or, sensible in all
things; show
ᵃ1 Tim. 5:1

to guard – ✱

⁷ ¹Or, soundness; lit,
uncorruptness
ᵃ1 Tim. 4:12

⁸ ²Thess. 3:14; 1 Pet. 2:12

⁹ ¹Lit, contradicting
ᵃEph. 6:5; 1 Tim. 6:1

to all men, bringing
᷾ Titus 1:3

᷾ Titus 3:4

ESSENTIAL PRINCIPLES

1

THE DIGNITY AND SANCTITY OF THE HOME
The Dignity and Sanctity of the Home Study Guide

2

THE ALSO PRINCIPLE
The Also Principle Study Guide

3

THE USE-WHAT-YOU-HAVE PRINCIPLE
The Use-What-You-Have Principle Study Guide

4

THE TABLE PRINCIPLE
The Table Principle Study Guide

THE DIGNITY AND SANCTITY OF THE HOME

"For this cause a man shall leave his father and his mother, and shall cleave to his wife; and they shall become one flesh."

GENESIS 2:24

The first institution that God established was the family. God established divine order in the first home, the Garden of Eden. He gave specific instructions to the first two homemakers, Adam and Eve, requiring them to be obedient. God had already set the family in order *before* giving the Law and before sending His Son to the cross. At the beginning of Jesus' ministry He performed His first miracle for a family when He changed the water into wine for the wedding at Cana in Galilee (John 2:1-11).

From Song of Solomon to the book of Revelation the Church is seen as "the Bride of Christ." The preeminence of the family is seen clearly in this expression. Since God chose the marriage relationship to portray our relationship with Him, then He obviously places high value and honor on the husband/wife relationship. Throughout Scripture we can see that God has conferred dignity and sanctity on the institution of the home.

WHAT IS MEANT BY "THE DIGNITY AND SANCTITY OF THE HOME"?

DIGNITY

The dignity of the home is seeing and experiencing its worth by those who are touched by it. Webster says dignity means "worthy of recognition due to a change in character and appearance." Combining *worth* with *character* and *appearance* defines dignity. A home that has dignity sets standards of order and creativity with the godly characteristics of love, honesty, and loyalty.

SANCTITY

The sanctity of the home is its purity in heart and purpose—its wholeness and holiness in tone and mood. Home is a duet of devotion and worth—devotion to God while valuing one another. Home is the sanctuary for the human soul to be recharged, renewed, refreshed and restored.

Read what other authors have said about the worth and the wholeness of the home to the human heart.

> *"When you make yourself at home, you surround*
> *yourself with the people you love,*
> *the objects you cherish, the memories that warm you,*
> *and the ideas that motivate you."*
>
> - EMILIE BARNES[1]

> Home is *"...the abiding place of the affections."*
> - ALEXANDRA STODDARD[2]

> *"When you keep house,*
> *you use your head, your heart,*
> *and your hands together to create a home—*
> *the place where you live the most important parts*
> *of your private life."*
>
> - CHERYL MENDLESON[3]

Home should be our most treasured asset. However, more and more women are devoting much of their energy to pursuits outside of the home. Unfortunately, the ambitions of "earning a higher education" and "pursuing a career" have undermined home values, priorities, and interests. Professional achievements do not change the fact that God designates women as the primary influencers in the home.

HOME IS THE BASIS FOR HUMAN SOCIETY

One of the most widely read books of all time is *The Decline and Fall of the Roman Empire.* In his book Edward Gibbon gives "Five Basic Reasons Why Great Civilizations Withered and Died". These are clearly as true today as when Gibbon wrote them in 1788.

1. The undermining of the *dignity and sanctity of the home,* which is the basis for human society. [Italics added for emphasis.]

2. Higher and higher taxes; the spending of public money for free bread and circuses for the populace.

3. The mad craze for pleasure; sports becoming every year more brutal, more immoral.

4. The building of great armaments when the real enemy was within—the decay of individual responsibility.

5. The decay of religion; faith fading into mere form, losing touch with life, losing power to guide the people.

HOME—THE BASIS FOR HUMAN DEVELOPMENT

Home has ceased to be the center of family activity. Day-care centers, baseball diamonds, football fields, basketball courts, and fast food restaurants have replaced it. Even excessive church activities can usurp the time that a family needs at home. I have known some church families whose weekly calendar looks like this: Sunday a.m.—service, Sunday p.m.—service, Monday p.m.—praise band practice, Wednesday p.m.—service, Friday p.m.—youth, and Saturday a.m.—leadership training. Each one of these activities is a good thing by itself. Some are even essential. However, not a single one or even all of these activities put together can replace the nurturing environment of a healthy home. *Who* one becomes is a direct reflection of *where* one spends most of his time.

HOME IS NOT AN ACTIVITY

Home is not an activity. Neither is it just a physical structure where a family dwells. It is intended to be a setting for the personal relationships of the members of a family. Home is the basis for human society. Few will argue that we don't need to improve the current condition of our society. Therefore, we can conclude that we must improve the condition of our homes.

A house becomes a home when people spend time together in it. Even a tent can become a home when the people that live in it are mutually building godly relationships. Hatred, anger, and chaos undermine dignity and sanctity because they tear down godly relationships. The atmosphere in a family dwelling determines the destiny of those who live there. When your family creates an atmosphere of love, joy, and peace, then you are making your home one of dignity and sanctity.

TWO ESSENTIAL HUMAN NEEDS—LOVE AND PEACE

Every human soul cries out for these essential needs: love and peace. When these two vital elements are not provided in the home, a life-long search begins which can take people into some very dark places. Because home is the central system in which human development occurs, the function of the home should be carefully designed. As families execute their plan to provide positive growth needed by each person living in that home, the result can be glorious.

CAREFUL DESIGN OF THE HOME

I have often said that I can determine a person's values by looking at her checkbook, her calendar, and her home. Regardless of what she says are her values, the truth is, the way that she spends her money and time and the manner in which she lives in her home reveal the things that truly are most important to her.

The design of your home (not the floor plan) should be intentionally programmed to ensure that priorities are instilled in the lives of family members. How your home is set up and what you do there will determine the outcome. For example, if you want a peaceful environment, then your home must have organization and order. If you want it to be comfortable, it must be furnished in a way that will cause people to want to relax. If you want your family to be industrious, you must assign responsibilities to each family member. If you want your home to express love, you must be willing to sacrifice your selfish goals and choose to put others before yourself. If you want your home to be hospitable, you must equip it for the comfort of the guests you plan to invite. If you want your home to bring honor to God, then you must acknowledge Him in all of your decisions.

ESTABLISHMENT OF FAMILY VALUES

Values are the things in your life that you think are important. Your list of values may include husband, children, friends, family, God, and work. Unfortunately, our "walk doesn't always agree with our talk." In other words, when we measure how we actually *live* by what we *intend,* we find that there is inconsistency. You may say, "Family is important", because you already know that family values bring health to a family. However, it is not enough to just say it. You must also create family time on your calendar and be willing to spend money on family activities.

RELATIONSHIPS REQUIRE TIME TOGETHER

Analyzing your list will also reflect the importance of the people in your life. Your choices of how you spend your time do not lie about your values. When you spend time together in your home, you must interact with one another. This interaction can be in conversation, recreation, or work. It can be a time of sharing the good things that have happened. It can be a time of healing. The loom of laughter, tears, consolation, and encouragement weaves together a tightly knit family. But this can only happen if you are at home and together.

BRING THE FRAGMENTED FAMILY BACK HOME

A lit candle on the counter, a fire in the fireplace, and the fragrant smell of stew simmering on the stove all say, "I'm here. I'm home." What else does it say? It says, "Come in, sit down, and talk to me. You are important and I want you here with me."

The table set with color and thought says, "Let's be face to face, share, talk, laugh and listen. Let's love each other." Even if there is only a simple bowl of beans to share, you can be rich in relationship. Home is not necessarily about what we have but how we use what we have.

ROOMS SPEAK

Creating a loving, peaceful atmosphere encourages family members to retreat *to* and not *from* the home. My daughter has four children. I have observed that the friends of her children are drawn to her home. Many of their friends have larger, fancier, and more expensive homes, but they prefer coming to my daughter's. The reason is simple. Kids are greeted with color, fun, and food whenever they enter my daughter's home. A snack sits on her counter beautifully displayed at all times. Her only living area is furnished with comfy sofas and chairs, ottomans, blankets and pillows. The room says, "Sit down, lie down, look at one another—talk, laugh, or sing. We want you here!"

Look at your home and ask, "What do my rooms say to people who enter?" Does the clutter say, "Go somewhere else! There is no space for you?" Does the formality say, "Sit up straight!" "Change your clothes!" "Be seen and not heard?" Does a cold stove say, "If you're hungry, get it yourself—I'm busy with more important things?" Do your children scatter to other homes in the neighborhood? Does your husband hurry home after work? Be brave and ask yourself: "What physical changes can I make in my home to create a more warm and inviting atmosphere?"

MARRIED OR SINGLE –YOU ARE THE "KEEPER"

Titus 2:3-5 clearly defines the responsibility that women have to relationally preserve feminine responsibilities and values. Each generation is to pass these teachings to the younger women. We are to teach them to love their husbands and to love their children, to be sensible, pure (in motive), keepers of the home, kind, and to be submitted to their husbands so the Word of God will not be dishonored.

I especially want you to notice the words *keepers at home* (King James version). What does this phrase mean? Some translations are limited to the idea of working at home. The Greek word is "oikouros". This word comes from two words: oikos which means "a dwelling"; and ouros meaning "to guard". So the woman is to guard her dwelling.

In practical terms it means that women are to be fully aware of all the activities that go on in her home. She is to guard the atmosphere that nothing will cause her to lose peace and love from the environment that she creates. Whether married or single, you have dominion over your environment. Keep peace with soft, gentle tones and keep love by always controlling your responses to consider others more important than yourself.

REFOCUS ON REBUILDING

Society's popular trends should never dictate what you do or don't do in your home. Within the law of the land and under God's Law, we have a higher mandate. The reason our lives have become so confused and anxiety-filled is that we have lost our focus on the worth and value God places on the home.

When women's hearts return to the home, society will improve. Families will be strengthened and neighborhoods will come to life. Porches will be swept and wreaths hung on doors. Perhaps, once again, children will play together in the yard and neighbors will know one another by name.

What will it take for your home to become a haven of peace and a sanctuary of love? What are you willing to do to restore the dignity and sanctity of your home so that the love of God and the peace of the Lord dwell in your home? Don't be overwhelmed. God will give you a plan.

A FUN AND ENLIGHTENING EXPERIMENT

I challenge you to do the following exercise to measure your true values. You may need to make some adjustments to your daily schedule. This can be a good place to begin to restore dignity and sanctity to your home.

Make a calendar of one week, recording the activities of each person in your family.

- Write down what every person does each day. Include the following:
  - appointments
  - activities
  - unstructured time (describe as "in front of TV", "on computer", "talking on phone", "play", "visiting friends")

- At the end of the week, create a chart of columns
  - Write one of your stated values at the top of each column
  - Leave a few columns blank (to be filled in during next step)

- Categorize and list each activity in the column with a corresponding value. Examples are listed below.

• Going to one's job	value is work
• Play	value is recreation
• Dining out with spouse	value is marriage
• Prayer, Bible, Church	value is spiritual growth

- Evaluate the outcome. Sample observations may include:
  - Too much *play* and too little work.
  - Too much *work* and not enough family time.
  - Too much *entertainment,* too little spiritual growth

- Share the results of your study with your family members.

Encourage change where it is needed. Bring integrity to your family as you work together to change your daily activities so that they reflect what you believe is important—better yet, what God says is important.

---

[1] Emilie Barnes: <u>Welcome Home</u>, Harvest House Publisher

[2] Alexandra Stoddard: <u>Creating A Beautiful Home</u>, Morrow Publisher

[3] Cheryl Mendleson: <u>HOME Comforts the Art and Science of Keeping House</u>, Scribner, Publisher

"A wise woman builds her house..."

Proverbs 14:1

YOUR HOME EXPERIENCE
STUDY GUIDE

The Dignity and Sanctity of the Home

PURPOSE: To restore greater value to your home and family life.

THE CONDITION OF OUR HOMES TODAY

(1) The underlying cause of society's decline has been the profound shift away from the value and purpose of the home. Our homes have ceased to be the center of our activities. Where are we spending most of our time?

_____

_____

_____

WHAT IS MEANT BY THE "DIGNITY AND SANCTITY" OF THE HOME?

Dignity refers to the value of a home both in physical appearance and in godly character of those who dwell there. Webster's dictionary defines dignity as "worthy of recognition due to a change in character and appearance."

A home with dignity sets standards of order and creativity in its physical presentation. Those who live in a home with dignity demonstrate the character traits of servanthood, sacrificial love, hospitality, determination, work ethic, submission, sensitivity, honesty, and loyalty.

Sanctity refers to "holiness" which is the purity in heart and purpose of the home. This core value develops an environment of wholeness—essential to the human soul.

Sanctity is from the Latin word "sanctus" which means "holy". Restoring the sanctity of the home deals with changing the tone and mood of your home. As women we set the tone and mood of our homes positively or negatively.

(2) Describe your home environment. Is it a haven of peace or a cave of confusion? Why?

_____
_____
_____

Remember that every home can use some improvements—minor or major. Restoring the *dignity and sanctity* of your home means to repair its broken and fragmented pieces. The restoration of wholeness in your home will begin by the choices you make.

(3) According to Edward Gibbon in his book *The Decline and Fall of the Roman Empire* (written in 1788), what is the first reason why great civilizations withered and died? Do you see how this is true in our society today?

_____
_____
_____

WE'VE BEEN TWEAKED

(4) In our society the value of the home has dramatically changed in the past two decades alone. Like being in a slowly revolving restaurant, you can look out after an hour or so and notice that the entire scenery has changed. I call this being tweaked or moved off course. What are some of the causes for this slow erosion of the home as the basis for human growth and development? Do you feel that this has happened to you? How?

_____
_____
_____

TRY THIS EXPERIMENT

Write down all the activities of each family member for one week. At the end of the week, create a chart with columns. Write one of your stated values at the top of each column. Leave some blank columns to be filled in during the next step. Afterwards, categorize each activity listed on your calendar and copy it in the corresponding column of your chart. Evaluate the outcome. Try to answer some of the following questions:

(5)   a. Do your activities support and help to accomplish your values? Or are your values undermined with busy activities.

_____
_____
_____

⑥   b.   Are there any adjustments that need to be made for a healthier home environment?

_____

_____

_____

    c.   After a time of prayer share your results with your family members.

YOUR HOME SPEAKS

⑦ Look at your home and ask yourself, "What do my rooms say to people who enter?" Does the clutter say, "Go somewhere else? There is no space here for you!" Does the formality say, "Sit up straight!" "Change your clothes!" "Be seen and not heard?" What message does your kitchen give? What area(s) of your home give a warm and inviting message? Which room(s) could use a make-over?

_____

_____

DEVELOP HEALTHY ATTITUDES

In order to develop healthy, balanced attitudes about change, remember that you are never alone. God will empower you to make healthy changes in your home. Understand that this transformation is a process. When you are trying to change bad habit patterns, you will make mistakes. You will do things without thinking. At such times, just pause and recognize, "Oh, my goodness! That's out of my old habit pattern." You then need to stop, think, and restate it or re-do it correctly.

⑧ My home will have greater dignity as I improve the appearance of it. What one physical improvement can I make this week to show greater value in my home?

_____

_____

_____

⑨ My home will have greater dignity when higher standards of character such as: love, honesty, loyalty are practiced. What one character trait can I focus on this week for myself and my family?

_____

_____

_____

⑩ Think of one thing you may be able to do this week to restore greater sanctity or wholeness to your home. In other words, how can you adjust the tone and mood of your home environment?

_____

_____

_____

_____

⑪ Guard the peace of your home. What personal changes need to be made in your own attitudes and speech for peace to come into your home?

_____

_____

_____

_____

STEPS TO TAKE

- Begin with prayer. *"Prayer is the foundation for all ministries."* ~ Larry Titus
- Make a list of the things in your life that have undermined the home.
- Repent for underestimating the importance of the atmosphere in your home.
- Learn everything you can about home care and develop these skills.
- Observe other families whose values you respect. Learn by observing their lifestyle.
- Rearrange your schedule so you can be at home more. Make home a priority!

> *"The wise woman builds her house, but with her own hands,*
> *the foolish one tears hers down."*
>
> PROVERBS 14:1

PRAY WITH A FRIEND

> *Confess your sins (faults, slips, gaps) to one another*
> *And **pray for one another** and you will be healed.*
> *The prayer of a righteous man is powerful and effective.*
>
> JAMES 5:16 AB

Activate your desires to improve by telling a friend about the changes that you want to make in your home environment. Now pray together and allow God to be powerful and effective in motivating you toward your new goals.

THE ALSO PRINCIPLE

"But I say to you, do not resist him who is evil;
but whoever slaps you on your right cheek, turn the other also."

MATTHEW 5:39 NASB

The Also Principle is demonstrated many times in scripture and always relates to character, obedience, and inheritance. It is manifested through our attitude and our willingness to serve others even when it is inconvenient. When the Also Principle is woven into our character and we are obedient to God's Word, we will experience God's blessings known as the "inheritance of Abraham."

So often the seemingly small things keep us from living a joyful and love filled life. We have simplified our lifestyles with modern conveniences such as fast-food, unmade beds, and hired help, yet life gets more complicated. Listen to your thoughts. Do you think any of the following?

- "Ah, that's good enough!"
- "That'll do."
- "Well, I've done all that I'm going to do!"
- "That's not my responsibility."

These kinds of attitudes indicate that you can improve your life by applying the Also Principle.

THE DIFFERENCE BETWEEN
AN INSTRUCTION AND A PRINCIPLE

Before I go further, let me explain to you the difference between a principle and an instruction. It would be much easier for me to tell you exactly what to do to assure you that your life has positive outcomes. But life does not work that way.

❧ An instruction tells you step by step how to do something. It is specific to a particular task. You usually can't apply it to the other areas of your life. For example, instructions on how to bake a cake cannot be used to instruct you on how to download software. Instructions do not use reason to accomplish a task. Just follow the instructions and do it like they tell you, and you will get the outcome whether you understand or not.

❧ A principle, however, is a truth that gives you the "why" and allows you to reason. Therefore, a principle can be applied to any or all areas of your life. For example, the principle of sowing and reaping is whatever you sow you will reap. Although that is a farming term, it is not telling you how to plant—that is an instruction. The principle is what you plant is what will grow.

Now, let's reason and apply the sowing and reaping principle to several areas of your life. If you sow kindness in relationships, you will receive kindness. If you sow money into a bank, you will receive money with interest from the bank. If you sow helping others, others will help you.

This chapter gives you truth that will impact many aspects of your life. The Also Principle will build your character in such a way that you become a *do-more* person rather than a *do-less* person. A *do-more* attitude will grow your faith, turn your provision into prosperity, propel you to live in obedience, and cause you to crave having an intimate relationship with God.

HERE IS HOW IT WORKS

The story recorded in Genesis 24:10-26 tells about Abraham sending his servant to his home country to select a wife for his son, Isaac. Why? He wanted to insure that Isaac's wife would have the qualities, character, and values that were traditionally a part of the training in his family—training that was apparently not seen in the Canaanite people among whom he was currently residing. Abraham needed to be assured that Isaac's wife would partner with his son to steward his inheritance.

The inheritance that he wanted to pass to his lineage included the following:

- Faith
- Provision
- Prosperity
- Obedience
- Intimacy with God

AN UNUSUAL PRAYER

After traveling with a team of 10 camels, Abraham's servant arrived at the town of Nahor at dusk, the time when women go out to draw water. He prayed for God to reveal who Isaac's wife should be. He asked God to cause the right woman to answer his request for water by saying, "Drink and I'll water your camels *also.*" By this he would know whom the Lord had selected for Isaac's wife.

ESSENTIAL CHARACTER

This was an interesting way to select one girl from a city of many. However, he knew that a young lady who was willing to draw 50 gallons of water for 10 camels, in addition to her routine chore of drawing water for her family, has character. When Rebekah did this, the servant then asked if he could go to her home to lodge. She quickly offered him the hospitality of her family. And as the story reads, she became Isaac's wife. Consider the character traits that qualified Rebekah to live in the blessings of Abraham's inheritance.

- Responsible
- Serving
- Industrious
- Courteous
- Charitable to strangers
- Willing to share
- Hospitable
- Finished what she started
- Submitted to the authority of her family

The Also Principle is defined by a willing attitude to do more than is asked of you. This attitude positions you to be sensitive to the needs of others and to be willing to go the extra mile—not one mile or two miles but whatever it takes.

The following are life areas where the scripture clearly talks about this principle.

THE ALSO PRINCIPLE IN YOUR WORK HABITS

"Whatever you do, do your work heartily (Greek "psuche") as for the Lord
rather than for men; knowing that from the Lord
*you will receive **the reward of the inheritance.***
It is the Lord Christ whom you serve."
COLOSSIANS 3:23-24 NASB (emphasis added)

"Psuche" is the Greek word that is variously translated as "mind," "soul," "breath," "heart," or "life." Colossians 3:23-24 is telling us to put our minds to whatever we do. Do not do your work with a halfhearted attitude but add the *also*.

- When it is time to leave work, stay a little longer—*also*.
- Clear your desk, dust it—*also*.
- Drive your car, clean it out—*also*.
- Take a shower, remove the hair—*also*.
- Wash your hands, dry the basin—*also*.
- When you wash the dishes, sweep the floor—*also*.

"But Zacchaeus stood up and said to the Lord,
'Look, Lord! Here and now I give half of my possessions to the poor,
and if I have cheated anybody out of anything,
I will pay back four times the amount.' Jesus said to him,
'Today salvation has come to this house,
because this man, too, is a son of Abraham. [The inheritance]
For the Son of Man came to seek and to save what was lost."
LUKE 19:8-10 (brackets and wording added)

The inheritance of Abraham, namely faith, provision, prosperity, obedience, and a relationship with God, came to Zacchaeus and his household because he was willing to give back more than what was expected—the *also*.

THE ALSO PRINCIPLE IN YOUR HOME

Jesus said, "If a slave comes in from work and sits at the table
and expects to be served without serving, he would not be thanked
for what he was supposed to do. But he should come in
and serve you after he has done his work."
LUKE 17:7-10

Everyone comes home after doing something that has consumed the best energy of his or her day. Most Moms and Dads arrive home from work, and the children come home from school. Everyone is tired, but dinner must be prepared, homework completed, and chores accomplished. Jesus clearly teaches that after we have done our work, we are still to serve one another. Here are a few simple *also* ideas for your home.

- When you set the table, light the candle *also.*
- When you wash and dry your laundry, fold it *also.*
- When you take a bath or shower, leave the tub clean *also.* Remove lingering hair with a damp tissue *also.*
- When you use the toilet, put down the lid *also.*
- When you undress, hang your clothing *also.*
- When you mow the lawn, edge it *also.*
- When you wash the dishes, dry them *also.*

THE ALSO PRINCIPLE IN YOUR SPEECH

"Be wise in the way you act toward outsiders;
make the most of every opportunity.
Let your conversation be always full of grace,
seasoned with salt, so that you may know
how to answer everyone."
COLOSSIANS 4:5-6

"Let your conversation be always full of grace, seasoned
with salt [also], so that you may know how to answer everyone."
COLOSSIANS 4:6 (brackets and word added)

Be a leader in conversation. Take initiative. To *"Let your conversation be always full of grace, seasoned with salt…"* means to give honor and favor to the person to whom you are talking. It is sad to observe how self-centered society has become. It is rare to encounter someone who takes initiative in meaningful conversation.

Our granddaughter, Brooke, at the age of seventeen began attending a very special theater school at the start of her high school senior year. She had attended a different school until this time, so, naturally, everyone was new to her. After her first day there, I asked her how things went. This was her reply. "It is great to be in a new environment where I do not know anyone. It is amazing how ill equipped people are to initiate conversation, so I take the responsibility to make it easier for them."

When you are in a group of people, do you take the responsibility to interact with them? Or, do your wait for them? Unfortunately we miss many awesome relational experiences by remaining to ourselves or by being satisfied with a mere cordial "hello."

Now read Matthew 5:38-48. Listed in this text are several *also* Scriptures. Consider these:

- Whoever slaps you on the cheek, turn the other *also.*
- If anyone wants to sue you, and take your shirt, let him have your coat *also.*
- Whoever shall force you to go one mile, go with him two *also.*
- Give to him who asks of you, and do not turn away from him who wants to borrow from you *also.*
- "You shall love your neighbor, and hate your enemy" was expected. But Jesus said to love your enemies, and pray for them *also.* Matthew 5:43-44

> *"For if you love those who love you, what reward have you?*
> *Do not even the tax-gatherers do the same?*
> *And if you greet your brothers only, what do you do more than others?*
> *Do not even the Gentiles do the same?*
> *Therefore you are to be perfect, as your heavenly Father is perfect."*
> MATTHEW 5:46-48 NASB

CONFRONT YOUR HINDRANCES

The character of Rebekah qualified her to inherit the blessings of Abraham and steward them for the next generation. So it can be with you. If you want to live in God's abundance in faith, provision, prosperity, obedience and in your relationship with Him, it is important to confront the hindrances that will keep you from serving others and obeying the Also Principle.

The following scriptures refer to the results of someone who is lazy and procrastinates, which is the opposite of the Also Principle. The scripture uses the term "sluggard." To be a "sluggard" is to be sluggish, to delay (procrastinate). As you read these verses from Proverbs, confront any sluggardly attitude or action in your life that may be hindering your blessing.

> *"How long will you lie down, O sluggard? When will you arise from your sleep?*
> *"A little sleep, a little slumber, A little folding of the hands to rest" – And your poverty*
> *will come in like a vagabond, And your need like an armed man.*
> PROVERBS 6:9-11 NASB

"The soul of the sluggard craves and gets nothing,
But the soul of the diligent is made fat."
PROVERBS 13:4 NASB

"The soul of the sluggard does not plow after the autumn,
So he begs during the harvest and has nothing."
[He doesn't finish what he starts!]
PROVERBS 20:4 NASB (words in bracket added)

"The desire of the sluggard puts him to death,
For his hands refuse to work; All day long he is craving,
While the righteous gives and does not hold back."
PROVERBS 21:25-26 NASB

"I passed by the field of the sluggard, And by the vineyard of the man lacking sense;
And behold, it was completely overgrown with thistles,
Its surface was covered with nettles, And its stone wall was broken down.
When I saw, I reflected upon it; I looked, and received instruction.
'A little sleep, a little slumber, A little folding of the hands to rest,'
Then your poverty will come as a robber,
And your want like an armed man."
PROVERBS 24:30-34 NASB

The key part of the verse for you in this final passage is: *"…I looked, and received instruction."* Begin applying the Also Principle in every area of your life. Make a list of the areas in your life that are like the "stone wall broken down." In a second column list the *also* that you can add to begin building up that broken down wall.

---

1 All scripture texts are quoted from the New American Standard Version.

"...you were faithful with a
few things, I will put you in charge
of many things, enter into the
joy of your master."

Matthew 25:21 NASB

YOUR HOME EXPERIENCE
STUDY GUIDE

The Also Principle

PURPOSE: To understand how the Lord's rewards are received and passed on in your life through the application of this biblical attitude.

WHAT IS THE ALSO PRINCIPLE?

The Also Principle is an attitude about everyday life that says, "I will do more than what is expected of me because I am working for the Lord. He will reward me." We believe that this attitude releases God's supernatural power and joy into every believer's life. In other words, when you do your work don't just do what is required of you. There is no special reward in that. Instead, make it a practice to go beyond without desiring praise or credit from people. Work as if God were your boss. This attitude will cause you to receive "the reward of the inheritance" mentioned in Colossians 3:23-24. God is the one who will reward you both now and in eternity.

① Have you ever made statements like the following? "Ah, that's good enough." "It will do." "I've already done more than what's expected. Now, I'm through!" "I'm tired, someone else can do this. Besides it's really not my job." What impact do you think such statements can have upon your family, friends, and co-workers?

_____

_____

The Also Principle was first established when Abraham sent his servant to find a wife for his son, Isaac. He was looking for a woman of suitable breeding and good character training. So Abraham sent his servant to look for a young lady from his own family line. (Genesis 24:1-20)

② Why did Rebekah stand out from among all the eligible single women? What did she also do when she met Abraham's servant at the well? What do you think you would have done in this situation?

_____

_____

③ Abraham was a man who practiced the Also Principle. This principle became a conduit for passing on the blessing of God to the next generation. What is meant by "the blessings" or "inheritance" of Abraham?

APPLYING THE ALSO PRINCIPLE AT WORK

Whether you are working at home or on the job, practice doing everything with excellence and for the glory of God. He will cause you to prosper in some way. Remember that there is no reward for doing only what is expected.

Please study the following key scripture verse. Ask God to give you insight and understanding for your own personal life.

> *"Whatsoever you do, do your work heartily*
> *as for the Lord rather than for men; knowing that from the Lord*
> *you will receive **the reward of the inheritance.***
> *It is the Lord Christ whom you serve."*
> COLOSSIANS 3:23-24 NASB (emphasis added)

④ The Greek word for working "heartily" is "psyche" (psoo-khay) which means with your mind, soul, breath, heart, and life. Think of any areas where you have had an attitude of "Well, that's good enough." How can you apply the Also Principle to your work?

As you know, everyone is required to be on time for work. The Also Principle would mean that you also arrive a little earlier than necessary and stay a little later. Don't be the first to rush out the door.

⑤ Other examples of this principle might include: Dusting your own desk when it is dirty. When using a public restroom, clean your hands and then, also wipe up the water off the sink. You can think of your own examples. What are some other ways that you can incorporate the Also Principle while working at you job or at home?

APPLYING THE ALSO PRINCIPLE AT HOME

Instead of just making the coffee, also serve the coffee. Take the coffee to your spouse with a napkin and a plate or coaster to set it on. Don't just make a meal and leave it on the stove for the family to help themselves, but also set the table. This could include: using place-mats, nice dishes, cloth napkins, and candles. Go one step further and put the food in serving dishes instead of bringing the pots and pans to the table. Adding these extra touches to enhance the meal not only incorporates this principle, but also makes your family will feel more valued and your table look better!

(6) Has God been speaking to you about your home? Is there a particular area you need to work on? If so, write down your ideas. For example, when you get dressed in the morning you can also make your bed neatly and place decorative pillows on it. After using the bathroom, also wipe the sink and clean the hair from the shower or tub.

_____

_____

_____

(7) Once you have a room looking neat and tidy ask yourself, "What special touch can also be added to improve the appearance and value?"

_____

_____

_____

APPLYING THE ALSO PRINCIPLE
IN YOUR RELATIONSHIPS

Make the most of your relationships. Even with new acquaintances. When you meet people, make an effort to learn their names. Write new names down for future reference along with an interesting fact or concern. Then, when you see them again, you can say their name and focus your conversation on them.

(8) Be sensitive to others. Make time for your relationships. Don't always be in a hurry. Stop, listen, and make eye contact. Is there someone that comes to your mind that you can apply this principle to? Describe one way that you can enhance that relationship.

_____

_____

_____

_____

⑨ The next time you are in the grocery store greet the cashier with a friendly "hello" and a smile. If she appears swamped with many customers, also bag your own order. When leaving the store, look at the cashier and also say to her, "Have a great day." Name another way that you can apply the Also Principle while you are out running errands.

_____

_____

_____

⑩ How can you apply this principle with those who are closest to you? Think of something you can do that would be unexpected and appreciated. Be sure not to imagine or calculate the response you desire to elicit. Remember, you are working for the Lord, not for people.

_____

_____

_____

ROBBERS OF YOUR INHERITANCE

Laziness is the opposite attitude of the Also Principle. It will weaken your faith, hinder your obedience, minimize God's provision for you, prevent prosperity from accumulating, and stifle your intimacy with God. It will prevent you and your family from experiencing all that God wants for you. Several passages of scripture share the common term, "sluggard." The definition of sluggard is "to be sluggish, to delay or to procrastinate." To be sluggardly is to be lazy.

⑪ Ask God to reveal one specific area of your life that He desires for you to redeem through the Also Principle. Write down practical changes you determine to make in your attitudes and actions. Make this declaration something that you can begin working on immediately. Don't allow yourself to be robbed of the Lord's blessings for one more day.

_____

_____

_____

_____

"You will eat the fruit of your labor;
blessings and prosperity will be yours."
PSALM 128:2

THE USE-WHAT-YOU-HAVE PRINCIPLE

"…you were faithful with a few things, I will put you in charge of many things, enter into the joy of your master."

MATTHEW 25:21

Matthew 25 teaches us about the Kingdom of God. It concerns the use of what you have been given for the benefit of the Kingdom. Jesus said:

> *Again, it [the Kingdom] will be like a man going on a journey,*
> *who called his servants and entrusted his property to them.*
> *To one he gave five talents of money, to another two talents,*
> *and to another one talent, each according to his ability.*
> *Then he went on his journey.*
> *The man who had received the five talents went at once*
> *and put his money to work and gained five more.*
> *So also, the one with the two talents gained two more.*
> *But the man who had received the one talent went off,*
> *dug a hole in the ground and hid his master's money.*
> *After a long time the master of those servants returned*
> *and settled accounts with them.*
> *The man who had received the five talents brought the other five.*
> *'Master,' he said, 'you entrusted me with five talents.*

See, I have gained five more.'

His master replied, 'Well done, good and faithful servant!

You have been faithful with a few things:

I will put you in charge of many things.

Come and share your master's happiness!'

The man with the two talents also came.

'Master,' he said, 'you entrusted me with two talents.

See, I have gained two more.'

His master replied, 'Well done, good and faithful servant!

You have been faithful with a few things:

I will put you in charge of many things.

Come and share your master's happiness!'

Then the man who had received the one talent came.

'Master,' he said, 'I knew that you are a hard man,

harvesting where you have not sown

and gathering where you have not scattered seed.

So I was afraid and went out and hid your talent in the ground.

See, here is what belongs to you.'

His master replied, 'You wicked, lazy servant!

So you knew that I harvest where I have not sown

and gather where I have not scattered seed?

Well then, you should have put my money on deposit with the bankers,

so that when I returned I would have received it back with interest.

Take the talent from him and give it to the one who has the ten talents.

For everyone who has will be given more,

and he will have an abundance.

Whoever does not have, even what he has will be taken from him.

And throw that worthless servant outside, into the darkness,

where there will be weeping and gnashing of teeth.'

MATTHEW 25:14-30

(bracketed words in verse 14 are added)

THREE MAIN POINTS

You can see in this passage that Jesus used the management of earthly assets to illustrate three central points:

1. The attitude that we should have toward the material possessions He has entrusted to us;

2. The responsibility we have to care for those possessions and to use them for His Kingdom; and

3. The end result of caring for them, depending on how we decide to manage and use them.

Let's consider these three aspects of what I call the *Use-What-You-Have Principle.*

FIRST POINT—YOUR ATTITUDE

In the above story, Jesus told of three servants whose master was preparing to go on a journey. The master entrusted a portion of his property to each servant according to that servant's ability. Two of the servants accepted their charge with a grateful and positive attitude. The third servant carried a negative attitude, apparently resentful over the master's assessment of his ability and the little that had been committed to him. Consequently, he failed to *use what he had,* to manage what he had, and to bless others with what he had.

When the master returned and asked for an accounting from the three servants, the one who had "buried his talent" and did not use it wisely responded very foolishly and angrily. In his bitterness he became irrational and defensive toward the one who had provided for him, blaming his master for his own unfruitfulness and unhappiness.

THE BEST POSSIBLE WAY The best possible way to *use what you have* is to share it with others. If you don't, you will find yourself with a negative outlook that will prevent you from enjoying your surroundings. This ungrateful attitude will stifle your creativity in using what you have in a fulfilling way. Your sense of personal fulfillment and self-respect relates commensurately with how you use what you have to bring life and joy to others.

RESULTS OF A NEGATIVE OUTLOOK Your attitude toward your home, your material possessions, your money, and your use of those things even affects your quality of life. An ungrateful heart often leads to disorder, confusion, and anger. An ungrateful heart and lazy attitude will steal your joy.

You can choose to be like the wicked, lazy servant. And you can choose to be irritated, believing that life has dealt unfairly with you. If you resent that you lack the "right" things or anything else you crave, then in discontent you will neglect to most effectively use what you already have.

SECOND POINT—YOUR RESPONSIBILITY

The story illustrates that our master will give us responsibility according to our ability. Our master, also, will return to see how we have managed and invested what he has committed to us. Our responsibility is to multiply what God has given to us for His Kingdom purposes. In the story, the rewards given to the faithful servants were great. The master said,

> *"Well done, good and faithful slave (servant);*
> *You were faithful with a few things, I will put you in charge of many things,*
> *enter into the joy of your master."*
> MATTHEW 25:21 NASB

Unfortunately for the one who had been irresponsible, the consequences were severe. Not only was he stripped of his talent (which was then given to the others who had demonstrated responsibility), but also, he was thrown "outside, into the darkness, where there will be weeping and gnashing of teeth." (Matthew 25: 30)

Joy, fulfillment, and prosperity are directly related to assuming the responsibility for multiplying what we have. The profits—material and spiritual—resulting from our proper management are not just ours alone. When we have been responsible with what is entrusted to us, our obedience is encouraging as well as beneficial to others. Building the Kingdom is giving others the life lessons which we learn from practicing Biblical principles.

Rather than using our own possessions by inviting others to our homes, we have expected the pastor or church leaders to practice hospitality for us. This is a charge therefore, to all believers to correct this thinking.

THIRD POINT—YOUR END RESULTS

Multiplication and fruitfulness are the rewards of gratefully sharing what you have with others and caring for what you have. You cannot rule that which you have not faithfully tended. The principle is clearly defined by the master in the following parable:

> *"You have been faithful with a few things: I will put you in charge of many things.*
> *Come and share your master's happiness!"*
> MATTHEW 25:21, 23

Your home, regardless of how simple or extravagant, must be used to its fullest potential for the Kingdom of God. Jesus said, "But seek first His kingdom and His righteousness, and all these things will be given to you as well." (Matthew 6: 33) The Greek word for "seek" is "ZETEO". It means "to desire earnestly" and "to strive after".

If you desire to have . . .

❧ the joy of the Lord flowing in your home

❧ your investments multiplied

❧ the reward of the Master

…then you must eagerly seek those things that build the Kingdom. Wisely use what you have to its maximum potential for the Kingdom of God.

If you are ungrateful, complaining about your lack and hoarding what little you do have, you will have no joy, prosperity, or fruitfulness. Your relationships will continue to be stressed, your misery will continue, and your frustration and lack will increase. Inevitably, the outcome will be loss of what you already have along with the heartache of seeing your things go to others who will both welcome and use them with grateful hearts. Even if they already have more! This was the scenario of the unfaithful steward who buried the money that his master had entrusted to him.

The choice is yours. What will you do with what you have?

APPLICATION

I am not insulted when I am invited into someone's home where the carpet shows signs of wear, the arms of the furniture are a bit soiled, and the serving dishes are chipped. Rather, it is a compliment to know that my hosts are sharing what they have. While I am with them, I will undoubtedly glean Kingdom principles from their character because I've looked for them.

ACTION LIST:

❧ Repent for an ungrateful heart.

❧ Repent for using your possessions only for yourself and your family.

❧ How can you improve what you have? Make an action list.

❧ To whom can you reach out, sharing what you have?

❧ Set a date to begin your changes to Use-What-You-Have.

When you begin to follow the path chosen by the two faithful servants, you will enter into the joy of the Lord as they did. Remember the promise of Jesus contained in this parable.

"Well done, good and faithful slave (servant);
You were faithful with a few things,
I will put you in charge of many things,
enter into the joy of your master."
MATTHEW 25:23 NASB

"This is what the LORD *says:*

Put your house in order..."

~ 11 Kings 20:1b

**YOUR HOME EXPERIENCE
STUDY GUIDE**

Use-What-You-Have Principle

PURPOSE: To motivate you to be faithful and trustworthy with all the resources and talents God has entrusted to you.

FOUNDATIONAL TRUTHS

The Bible is our road map for healthy living. It is filled with truths that will transform your life. The Use-What-You-Have Principal comes from the Parable of the Talents in Matthew 25:14-30. This parable describes the three servants who were each entrusted with a portion of his master's assets. The two who were diligent and trustworthy were rewarded with more talents. The ungrateful and pessimistic servant was judged by his master. What had been entrusted to him was taken away and given to one of the faithful servants.

① What do you notice about the attitudes of the three servants?

_____
_____
_____
_____
_____
_____
_____

② The third servant is called wicked and lazy by his master. Who did the servant blame for his own lack of responsible stewardship of the money? Have you ever felt like blaming others for your own actions?

_____
_____
_____
_____
_____
_____
_____

YOUR ATTITUDE

③ Your quality of life is largely impacted by your attitudes. An ungrateful heart attitude will steal your joy and rob you of blessings. Choosing to maintain a grateful attitude will motivate you to *Use-What-You-Have* to bless others.

Think about your attitude toward your own talents and abilities. Are you grateful or ungrateful? How does your attitude about yourself affect your obedience to God?

_____

_____

_____

_____

_____

④ Changing your attitude will change your destiny. A healthy attitude starts with a choice to be thankful. Think of an area of your life where you have neglected to be thankful. Ask God to show you any adjustments that you need to make.

_____

_____

_____

_____

_____

YOUR RESPONSIBILITY

⑤ The challenge is to *Use-What-You-Have* whether you're at home, church, or at work. For example, your home—big or small—is to be well cared for and used to its fullest potential for the Kingdom of God. The Lord, our Master, gives each one of us different levels of responsibility—each according to his/her ability. Then, He tests us to see if we will be trustworthy with the little things He calls us to do.

What if the Lord were to visit your home today? Would He see that you have managed and wisely invested what He has entrusted to you?

_____

_____

_____

_____

_____

YOUR END RESULTS

⑪ The principle is clearly defined in the verse below. The two servants mentioned in the parable of the talents who faithfully tended their master's assets were praised, rewarded, and experienced the joy that comes from a job well done.

> *You have been faithful with a few things: I will put you in charge of many things.*
> *Come and share your master's happiness.*
>
> MATTHEW 25:21, 23

Ask God to show you any area(s) of your life that He wants you to take better care of. Focus on one area that you can apply the Use-What-You-Have Principle to this week.

What specific change(s) do I need to make in regards to:

a. My home

_____

_____

_____

_____

_____

b. My relationships

_____

_____

_____

_____

_____

c. My _____(you fill it in)

_____

_____

_____

_____

_____

> *"Do not be deceived: God cannot be mocked. A man reaps what he sows."*
>
> GALATIANS 6:7

"I seek you with all my heart; do not let me stray from your commands. I have hidden your word in my heart that I might not sin against you."

~ Psalms 119:10-11

THE TABLE PRINCIPLE

*"She has prepared her meat and mixed her wine;
she has also set her table."*

PROVERBS 9:2

THE CLIMATE OF TODAY'S HOME

The typical family no longer eats meals together at the table. Parents sometimes get home late and are tired after working long hours and fighting traffic. Children are often left to feed themselves. Many families frequently resort to fast food in the car as a quick solution to their hunger pains. If family members are home at the same time, they often eat while watching television, reading the newspaper, or doing homework.

The table has been replaced by breakfast bars, fast food restaurants, coffee shops, drive through windows, and microwave mini meals where children often serve themselves and eat alone. In short, mealtime is no longer an opportunity for families to build relationships.

The Table Principle will show you the dramatic impact that simply sharing a meal can have on the most important people in your life. Your family will reap the rewards of choosing to adjust your busy lifestyle in order to join with those you love around your table.

The Table Principle is a truth that transcends culture and time. Since the creation of the first table, the table has been of primary importance to the family system. This principle stands true even when values shift and lifestyles change. Time spent at the table satisfies a cry of the human heart because a lovingly prepared table is a place where the presence of God dwells and individual relationships are established.

RESEARCHERS POINT TO THE FAMILY TABLE

Researchers speak of a common factor that has undermined the well-being of our young people. The missing element in our families is that our lifestyles no longer make room for eating meals together regularly.

The American Psychological Association published a study that illustrated the crucial role of the family meal in the lives of teenagers. The study found that adjusted teens—those with better relationships with their peers, more academic motivation, and few, if any, problems with drugs and depression—ate dinner with their families an average of five days a week.[1]

Dr. Chris Stout, former president of the Illinois Psychological Association and Chief of Psychology at Forest Hospital in Des Plaines, IL, points to the organized family meal's main ingredient—communication—as one key to raising emotionally healthy children. Tricky subjects, such as problems with peers or schoolwork, are more easily approached across the dinner table.[2]

Other research by the University of Minnesota and the University of North Carolina showed similar findings: "drug use, sex, violence and emotional stress were less likely in households where the parents were present at crucial times, particularly during meals."[3]

Why is eating at the table so important? This question prompted me to conduct a biblical search of the word table. I discovered profound answers to my question.

THE SIGNIFICANCE OF THE TABLE

GOD DESIGNED THE FIRST TABLE

God instructed Moses to have his people "make a sanctuary for me, and I will dwell among them." He told them to make this tabernacle and all its furnishings "exactly like the pattern I will show you." God gave Moses the details for building the Ark of the Covenant and then instructed him to make a table. The table as we know it today is the same design as the one built for the tabernacle. See Exodus 25:8-9.

After the table was built, God told Moses to make its plates and dishes of pure gold, as well as its pitchers and bowls for the pouring out of offerings.

> *"Make a table of acacia wood…*
> *And make its plates and dishes of pure gold,*
> *as well as its pitchers and bowls*
> *for the pouring out of offerings."*
>
> EXODUS 25:23, 29

THE BREAD OF THE PRESENCE

God told Moses to build this table and to set the table with plates, dishes, pitchers, and bowls which is similar to a dinner table. He further instructed him to…

> *"Put the bread of the Presence on this table to be before me at all times."*
>
> EXODUS 25:30

What is the bread of the *Presence?* In the New Testament Jesus referred to himself as the bread of life. (John 6:48) When family and friends gather around a prepared table, there is a supernatural presence that penetrates and strengthens relationships. The Presence at the table is Jesus—the bread of life. He promises that if we will open the door of our hearts to him he will come and dine with us. Jesus said,

> *"Here I am! I stand at the door and knock.*
> *If anyone hears my voice and opens the door,*
> *I will come in and **eat with him, and he with me."***
>
> REVELATION 3:20

THE TABLE PRINCIPLE IN ACTION

Scripture indicates many benefits of eating at the table. Here are a few illustrations when eating at the table made a difference in the lives of those who were invited to the table. Each illustration demonstrates the life-changing impact that was accomplished while at the table.

REPLACE THE PAIN OF REJECTION WITH CONFIDENCE AND PERSONAL VALUE…AT THE TABLE.

King David honored his covenant with Jonathan by restoring to Mephibosheth all the land that belonged to Saul and elevating him by saying to him, *"…you will always eat at my table."* 2 Samuel 9:7

After the untimely death of Jonathan, King David sought for a way to honor the covenant he had made with his friend. Jonathan's crippled son, Mephibosheth, was invited to dine at the King's table. David said to him *"…you will always eat at my table."* Mephibosheth had referred to himself as "a dead dog", unworthy of even being noticed. But David gave him a new sense of personal value when he treated him as a son by including him at his table.

Invite to your table someone who has been rejected and feels unworthy and allow supernatural love to touch their heart. His presence will restore them. All you have to do is prepare the table.

HONOR THOSE YOU PREVIOUSLY JUDGED

The evil king of Babylon released the king of Judah after 37 years of imprisonment. He restored his honor and dignity as a king by including him at his table.

> *"So Jehoiachin put aside his prison clothes*
> *and for the rest of his life ate regularly at the king's table."*
> II KINGS 25:29

When you have wrongly accused someone and ostracized them from your life, bring them to your table as a sincere act of restitution. This demonstration of love is more effective in bringing restoration than merely saying, "I'm sorry."

RESTORE FAMILY RELATIONSHIPS

The table played a significant role in restoring the prodigal son. His father announced, "Let's have a feast and celebrate." (Luke 15:23b) This father celebrated the son's homecoming without assigning blame or shame for what his son had done in the past. Did his father know what their future would hold? No. However, the father's embrace and decision to have a celebration feast gave his wayward son hope for a new future.

Prepare dinner for your grown children who have made horrible, wrong choices. The table is the best place to express your love. Create a loving environment at the table for them. The presence of the Lord and the love you share will help restore them.

INVITE THE OUTCASTS

> *"…a woman came to him with an alabaster jar of very expensive perfume,*
> *which she poured on his head as he was reclining at the table."*
> MATTHEW 26:7

Jesus was at the table of Simon, the leper, when this woman came into the house. Lepers lived as outcasts in communities outside of the city and were not allowed to enter the city.

Jesus went out to Simon's house for a meal and while eating at Simon's table an unworthy woman came to express her love for Jesus by pouring expensive perfume on his feet.

Extend yourself beyond your own neighborhood and go to those who would never expect you to sit at their table. They will feel honored by your expressions of love just like Simon and this woman did with Jesus. Who can you bring hope to by visiting them on the other side of town?

IT IS WISDOM TO PREPARE MEALS

"She has prepared her meat and mixed her wine;
she has also set her table."

PROVERBS 9:2

Who is "she" in this passage? *Wisdom.* The text tells us that it is wisdom to think in advance about what a family will eat for a meal. In addition to planning a meal, stopping at the grocery store or the local delicatessen if it is a busy day, it is also wisdom to set the table in advance so your meal will not be so hurried.

OTHER IMPORTANT VERSES

"Your wife will be like a fruitful vine in your house
and your sons will be like olive shoots around your table."

PSALM 128:3

"You have prepared a table before me in the presence of my enemies."

PSALM 23:5

Continue your own study, looking up verses that include the word table or other synonyms such as: banquet, eat, dine, and supper. You will discover that this is a very substantial subject in the Bible yet seldom does a pastor preach a sermon on the importance of the family table. Much of the time that Jesus spent teaching his disciples was around the table.

THE TABLE—A PLACE OF NEGOTIATION

Governments of the world negotiate peace and declare war at tables. Corporate destinies are determined at boardroom tables. The following are ideas of how you can benefit from the several ways the table can be used in your personal negotiations.

1. Negotiate marriage conflict at the table.

   When relational disappointments, instructions, or corrections need to be discussed between partners, the best place to discuss issues that need to be resolved is at the table without the children present. Go to dinner or prepare dinner at home around the table. Your body language will be more controlled and chances are better that you will engage in deeper conversation than if you talk anywhere else.

2. Negotiate parent/teen conflict at the table.

   When you need to get to the bottom of an issue with your teenager, you should talk to him or her at the table. The parent is more likely to be calm and the teen is less likely to storm out of the room. The parent has a greater opportunity to bring the conversation to a conclusion.

3. Hold family meetings at the table.

   Set family financial goals around your table. Include all family members in these discussions. When there is a need to prepare your family for family budget cutbacks, it is best to discuss it eye-to-eye around your table.

BENEFITS OF EATING AT THE TABLE— EXPERIENCE THE WORK OF HIS PRESENCE

We have already established that many positive benefits can be identified when the practice of eating at the table is closely examined. This practice positively affects a person's character as well as the stability of his emotions. There also remains an element of mystery that cannot be described.

Even after close examination of the practice of eating together at the table, there remain indescribable elements concerning this principle. Although researchers acknowledge that eating at the family table is important for various reasons, they cannot fully explain why it makes such a difference in a person's life. This leads me to the conclusion that there is an element of the supernatural—the work of His presence.

Following is a list of some of the wonderful benefits of eating at the table.

- Love is expressed.
- The Lord is honored.
- Character is developed.
- The physical body is better nourished.
- Training is experienced in a natural way.
- Children practice sharing and self-control.
- Family members learn to serve one another.
- Conversational skills are practiced and refined.
- Respect is shown for one another as good manners are practiced.
- Daily schedules can be discussed bringing order to family planning.
- Gratefulness, praise, and appreciation for each other can be shared.
- The practice of proper table manners prepares children for adulthood.

EATING ALONE?

The table is not just a place for parents and children. It is also a place where an unmarried man or woman can be touched by the Lord's presence. Do not always eat on the run or in front of a television. Treat yourself by setting your table, lighting a candle, turning on uplifting music, and relaxing in His presence while you eat. Even though you are single or eat meals alone, get into the habit of setting your table and communing with the Lord. What refreshing times you will have.

CAN'T WE JUST STAY HOME?

A five-year-old boy was dragging his coat across the yard while his impatient and hurried Mom was honking the horn. His older brothers and sister made it to the van before his little legs could get him there. They were late as usual and had to deliver his brothers to one baseball field and his sister to another. Mother yells one last time, "Hurry up Johnnie, we're going to be late!" In frustration, Johnnie desperately pleads, "Mom, can't we just stay home?"

Does this sound familiar? How will we hold our families together? Stay home more often and eat meals together around a table. Is it possible to be home one, two, or three nights a week? If evenings will not work for your schedule, then have breakfast together. Simply be willing to make adjustments and sacrifices to share meals together.

THE LIE VS. THE TRUTH

The lie that we have believed is that where we eat, how we eat, or what we eat is not important. Our rationale goes something like this: "All that matters is that we are together."

The truth is that it does matter that we are together. It also matters that we make it a practice to eat around a table together. What other normal activity provides opportunity for quality conversation, laughter, and learning from one another?

What we eat matters also. The brain is the central system of the human soul, containing the thinking and feeling capacity of a person. If it is not well fed, it will not develop to its full potential. How is it that we can justify feeding our toddlers pizza, coke, wieners, and hamburgers when just a few months earlier we gave them the essential nutritious fruits, grains, and vegetables from the baby food jars?

We wonder why school test scores are decreasing and the ability for a child to focus his attention is challenged. Can it be that the human brain is not getting the nourishment that is needed for learning?

AS OFTEN AS YOU EAT…REMEMBER ME

During the meal known as the Last Supper, Jesus and the disciples were reclining at the table. He took the bread, gave thanks and broke it. Then He passed it to them saying,

"This is my body given for you; do this in remembrance of me."
After dinner He took the cup, saying,
"This cup is the new covenant of my blood…"
LUKE 22:19-20

Did Jesus mean for us to simply make this a communion event once a month in our church gatherings? No. He was demonstrating the frame of mind that we should have at the table. As often as you eat *at the table* or as often as you eat dinner, remember the price that Jesus paid for you. Remember Him as you break bread together in your homes, especially among believers.

THE TABLE PRAYER

While it is essential to thank God for the food we eat, it is even more important to remember the price Jesus paid for us. Perhaps your table prayer could sound something like this:

Thank you, Father, for sending your son so that my family and I can have eternal life. May we never forget the price Jesus paid so that we can be forgiven of all our sins. We choose to honor you by loving each other as we share this time together. We are very grateful for our food and all of your wonderful provisions. Amen.

When you pray at your table, try using content similar to the prayer above. Choose your own words that are age appropriate to those who are around your table. If your children are young and you use the term Redeemer, you may want to explain what that word means as you are eating. Get your children's input on what they think it means. Table conversation should be a discussion rather than a lecture. Keep your terms simple and non-religious.

God's promise to you is that the bread of the Presence will dwell in your midst as you enjoy one another around your table. Supernatural experiences will happen in a natural way in the hearts of those who eat at your prepared table. Only time or eternity will reveal all of the eternal results of your sharing in the Lord's presence.

DEVI'S FAMILY TRADITIONS

Growing up I remember our dinner table was set for four or more—usually more. At the head of the table sat Daddy. Mother sat on the side to his right. My older brother and I usually sat to Daddy's left—first my brother, then me. The two extra chairs were in place and we could easily add two more plates. People always stopped by, and, if we were eating, they were invited to join us. They usually accepted our invitation.

Before a meal, Daddy would announce, "Let's all pray." It was at the table that I learned to pray aloud. I did not pray alone, but along with everyone else simultaneously. Our prayer was not memorized, neither was it the same every meal. My brother and I learned to imitate the expressions of our parents' grateful hearts.

MY FATHER'S FAMILY TABLE

Daddy was reared in a large family of ten children on a small farm in southeastern Oklahoma. It was the early part of the twentieth century. The family was very poor. I asked him how it was that he had such good character with such a difficult childhood. His answer was, "We didn't have things or education, but we had love. And Mama always had a meal on the table." They always ate at the table in a house that was quite small for this family of twelve. In spite of crowed space and shared beds, there was room for the all-important table.

Something supernatural transpired in the souls of this poor family while eating together more than once a day. It was at this prepared table that their character was being shaped. The security of love was being deeply embedded in their emotions. While the children were arguing over who would get the final serving of corn, they already had learned to share.

Everyone had a portion. The older helped the younger as they washed dishes together. They learned responsibility. All of them, including my grandparents, eventually committed their lives to Christ.

MY MOTHER'S FAMILY TABLE

Grandpa was clearly the head of the household in Mother's family. At the death of his father, he assumed the responsibility of providing for his mother and younger siblings as well as his wife and five children. They all lived together. Grandpa farmed and worked on state road construction.

Their table was large and fed many people. They also lodged visiting preachers and travelers. They were hospitable to neighbors on nearby farms. Their table included prayer, meals, laughter, instruction, bible studies and family games. It was the center of their home activity. Character, courage, and discipline were demonstrated around their table. Faith, hope and love were given to everyone who shared meals with them.

As you can see, Mother's family table was very different from Daddy's family table. However, the results of regularly eating together at their tables led to similarly healthy children.

OUR FAMILY TABLE

Seldom do Larry and I visit our adult children's homes that they do not have someone there for dinner. Sometimes I think, I wish we could just visit them without others here. But then I remember this is the way our family table was when they were growing up. Why should I expect anything different? Their family tables are places of joy and refuge for others in the same way ours was.

When the children were young, I prepared our table on Saturday night and we always brought a family home for dinner after church on Sunday. All holiday tables included others who had no special place to go. Men from prison, teens from the streets, celebrities, preachers, missionaries, relatives, parishioners—you name them, and they have probably eaten at our table. Larry often brought folks home with him for dinner with or without advance notice. This was our way of life.

Our children learned to serve others, to be courteous, and to converse with adults. It was later in our son's adult life that I asked him, "What impacted you the most while growing up in our home?" He quickly replied, "Oh that's easy Mom. It was the people that you had in our home!" I did not realize that I was shaping his Godly character at our table.

Both Aaron and Trina are hospitable and use their homes to love people and allow God to work in their lives while serving them a meal, a bowl of popcorn or a simple glass of tea. Presently, we see these same hospitable values repeated in the home of our adult granddaughter and her husband. Our way of life has become their way of life—giving life to others from our families' tables.

MAKE ROOM FOR HIS PRESENCE

Is it possible that the simple act of eating together at the table can begin a supernatural work in your family? Is it possible that the move of God that you have desired will happen as you sit with your family at the table in your home?

Dads will have to come home from work. Moms will need to prepare menus in advance. Children will need to help set the table and clear the table, and everyone should quickly do the dishes together. This is a family affair. Whether you are married, single, with children, or without children, *the bread of the Presence* wants to meet with you at your table.

Is it possible that Jesus wants to dine with you at your table, but He cannot because your life has become so absorbed in other things? Are you so busy going here and there, that you no longer come to the table where the King of kings and Lord of lords would like to join you? Is He knocking at your door, but you are too distracted to hear Him? Open the door, prepare your table, and allow His presence to dine with you.

Recently I have heard several instances of those whose age is over 30 who have never eaten a meal at a table in their homes. This may seem shocking but after speaking on The Table Principle in women's conferences, I sometimes have ladies informing me that they do not even have a table in their homes. In all such cases I learn that their relationships are strained, shallow, and unfulfilling. They tell me that their children are not at peace—neither are they flourishing. Why not begin again today? All you must do is *come to the table.*

CHECKLIST FOR RETURNING TO THE TABLE
MAKE THE TABLE A PRIORITY

- Repent to the Lord for compromising this valuable principle and begin making changes in your priorities.

- Clear the table of clutter. Stop using it as a drop off point for everyone to stash their stuff.

- Increase the number of meals you eat together. Not every meal has to be eaten around a table. For example, eating pizza while watching a football game or enjoying a good movie is a great way to have family time occasionally.

MAKE THE TABLE A PLACE OF PLEASURE

- Play a CD while dining as background music.

- Always edify one another while sitting at your table.

- Use your best dishes for your family so that they feel just as important as any special guest.

- Prepare meals that your husband likes. Include nutritious foods like fresh vegetables. This causes children to experience foods that they may not choose. Have them taste new foods.

- Include someone else at your table at least once a week. For example, invite a child's friend, a relative, a lonely single person, an unsaved friend or co-worker.

MAKE THE TABLE A PLACE OF PARTICIPATION

- When you unload the dishwasher, set your table in advance for the next meal that you will serve. Employ the help of children and teens in this process.

- Be practical. Even simple and quick preparation can be special. Ask for help in setting the table with colorful paper plates, napkins, and plastic ware.

- Flowers and a lighted candle always add a special touch.

---

1 Bryan, Catherine A. Frequency Of Family Meals May Prevent Teen Adjustment Problems. American Psychological Association. 8 August, 1997.

2 Figg, Erinn. Return to the Family Meal: Eating Together Puts Communication Back on Your Menu. 19 June, 2000.

3 ibid.

YOUR HOME EXPERIENCE
STUDY GUIDE

The Table Principle

PURPOSE: To understand the supernatural impact that sharing a meal together has on each family member's character, confidence, and self image.

THE CLIMATE OF TODAY'S HOME

(1) As you are probably aware many families no longer eat meals together at the table on a regular basis. Busy lifestyles and other reasons have contributed to this dilemma. Has your table been replaced by breakfast bars, fast-food restaurants, or simply eating on the run? Describe what mealtime is like for you and your family.

_____

_____

_____

_____

THE SIGNIFICANCE OF THE TABLE

(2) Moses received specific instructions for building the Tabernacle. God also gave explicit directions for furnishings for the table. Please read Exodus 25:23-30. What is the significance of the bread of the Presence?

_____

_____

_____

_____

(3) Jesus is described in John 6:48 as "the bread of life." Have you ever experienced the supernatural presence of the Lord at a set table when family or friends have gathered? Please relate your experience.

_____

_____

_____

_____

THE TABLE PRINCIPLE IN ACTION

④ The following scriptures describe the many benefits of eating at the table. Take a close look at these examples. Can you envision your table being a place of restoration and love?

1. Restore confidence and personal value—II Samuel 9
2. Honor those you previously judged—II Kings 25:29
3. Share your table, then your faith—Acts 2:46-47
4. Restore family relationships—Luke 15:23
5. Invite the outcasts—Matthew 26:7
6. Negotiate your differences at the table—Psalms 23:5

BENEFITS OF EATING AT THE TABLE

⑤ As you can see from reading this chapter there are many benefits of eating at the table. Has eating at the table been a high value of yours? _____

What are some benefits you see for eating meals together in your home?

_____
_____
_____
_____
_____
_____
_____

THE LIE VS. THE TRUTH

⑥ We have believed the lie that where we eat, how we eat, or what we eat is not important. We even rationalize by saying, "All that matters is that we are together." Please comment on this. What do you think? Has this lie infiltrated your home and family life?

_____
_____
_____
_____
_____
_____
_____
_____

EATING ALONE

⑦ The table is a place where the presence of the Lord dwells. His presence is there whether you are eating alone or in the company of others. You may be single, married, widowed, or divorced and find yourself eating many meals alone. What can you do to invite the presence of the Lord into your life during mealtime?

_____

_____

_____

_____

_____

_____

_____

A CHECKLIST FOR RESTORING THE TABLE

⑧ Look at the checklist in the book and write down practical ways you can make use of your table during this next couple of weeks.

_____

_____

_____

_____

_____

_____

_____

CREATING FAMILY TRADITIONS

⑨ Traditions can be established at any time. The first step is planning. The second step is getting started. Then, repeat what works and what you enjoy. What ideas do you have for instituting traditions during you family's table times? Reread Devi's family traditions to give you some new ideas.

_____

_____

_____

_____

_____

_____

_____

"*She has prepared her meat and mixed her wine; she has also set her table.*"

Proverbs 9:2

VITAL RELATIONSHIP SKILLS

5

PERSONALITY DYNAMICS
Personality Dynamics Study Guide

6

REDUCING FAMILY CONFLICTS
Reducing Family Conflicts Study Guide

7

HONORING YOUR HUSBAND
Honoring Your Husband Study Guide

PERSONALITY DYNAMICS

"May the Lord make your love increase and overflow for each other…"

I THESSALONIANS 3:12

The cry of every human heart is to experience peaceful and loving relationships. You can play a major role in building healthy relationships as you gain more knowledge of personality dynamics. Remember that God wants to impact others with His love through the personality He has given to you.

SENSITIVITY TO OTHERS

Here are three tips that will be helpful as you begin

- Be careful about categorizing family members. Remember, impulsive judgments can be wrong. Instead, make it your aim to develop a sincere appreciation for all personality blends in your family.
- Do not use this information to indulge in your own weaknesses. Statements like, "I can't help myself. This is just the way I am." should not be made.
- Never expose the weaknesses of other family members, especially in public. This thoughtless gesture can humiliate a child or spouse and actually hinder his growth.

YOUR MAKE-UP

Personality, life experiences, family background, intelligence, culture, society, religious beliefs, upbringing, and character traits all influence how we behave. Behavior style refers to how we act in different situations and settings.

The greatest impact on behavior is our God given personality. Each one of us has been *"fearfully and wonderfully made"* according to God's awesome plan as stated in Psalms 139. It is up to each of us to operate out of the strengths of our personality and not our weaknesses.

> *"For you created my inmost being;*
> *you knit me together in my mother's womb.*
> *I praise you because I am fearfully and wonderfully made;*
> *your works are wonderful, I know that full well."*
>
> PSALM 139:13-14

THE DISC PERSONALITY STYLES

There are four basic personality styles described in this next chart. Most people are a blend of two or three styles. As you read the descriptions below you may see yourself in one, two, or possibly three areas. Start by identifying your personality strengths and limitations. Then, see if you can identify other family members.[2]

Your relationships will improve as you:

1. Discover the personality styles in your home.
2. Adjust your own behavioral style to compliment others.
3. Enhance communication skills with words that edify others.
4. Reduce areas of conflicts. This topic is covered in the next chapter.

THE DISC PERSONALITY STYLES

FAST PACED ~ OUTGOING

DIRECT, DECISIVE, DOMINANT

CHARACTERISTICS	*LIMITATIONS*
___ Task focused	___ Impatient
___ Quick thinker	___ Blunt
___ Confident	___ Domineering
___ Born leader	___ Tactless
___ Positive	___ Bossy
___ Powerful	___ Competitive
___ Self-sufficient	
___ Goal oriented	
___ Bottom line leader	
___ Sees the whole picture	

The Doer

INSPIRATIONAL, INFLUENTIAL, INTERACTIVE

CHARACTERISTICS	*LIMITATIONS*
___ People focused	___ Talks too much
___ Articulate	___ Disorganized
___ Enthusiastic	___ Not detailed
___ Charming	___ Undisciplined
___ Fun loving	___ Emotional
___ Energetic	___ Forgetful
___ Spontaneous	
___ Demonstrative	
___ Communicator	
___ Impulsive	

The Talker

CONSCIENTIOUS, CORRECT, CREATIVE

CHARACTERISTICS	*LIMITATIONS*
___ Task focused	___ Critical
___ Deliberate paced	___ Feels pressured
___ Creative	___ Judgmental
___ Serious	___ Perfectionist
___ Analytical	___ Suspicious
___ Sensitive	___ Worrisome
___ Scheduled	
___ High standards	
___ Artistic/Musical	
___ Genius prone	

The Thinker

STEADY, STABLE, SENSIBLE

CHARACTERISTICS	*LIMITATIONS*
___ People focused	___ Indecisive
___ Deliberate paced	___ Resists change
___ Faithful	___ Unenthusiastic
___ Peacemaker	___ Indifferent
___ Listens well	___ Hides feelings
___ Loyal	___ Holds grudges
___ Calm	
___ Sympathetic	
___ Highly relational	
___ Dry sense of humor	

The Watcher

TASK FOCUSED

PEOPLE FOCUSED

SLOW PACED ~ RESERVED

SIMILARITIES IN PERSONALITY
FOCUS AND PACE

Some personalities are naturally focused on projects, whereas others are more focused on relationships. One is not better than the other. Your unique blend of personality styles could cause you to focus on both tasks and people.

Pace has to do with the speed at which we think, respond, and live. Some people tend to move at a fast pace while others move at a slow pace.

HOW TO BUILD CLOSER RELATIONSHIPS

God is more interested in how we treat each other than in who is right or wrong. This section will give you great insight into specific ways to improve your relationships. Practice making modifications in your personality style to meet the needs of others. I believe that this is the secret behind Paul's ability to spread the gospel to many different groups of people.

> *"Though I am free and belong to no man,*
> *I make myself a slave to everyone,*
> *to win as many as possible.*
> *To the Jews I became like a Jew, to win the Jews*
> *. . . to the weak I became weak, to win the weak.*
> *I have become all things to all men so that by all possible means*
> *I might save some."*
> I CORINTHIANS 9:19-22

MODIFICATIONS FOR THE DIRECTIVE D
- Slow your pace. Talk and move a bit slower.
- Be quick to say, "I'm sorry, I was wrong."
- Practice patience and listening. Don't give advice when not asked.
- Spend quality time on your important relationships.
- Don't allow work or projects to be a higher priority than people.
- Be quick to give praise and affection to those around you.
- Soften your voice, your words, and your approach.
- Relax: try not to control or dominate situations in your home.

MODIFICATIONS FOR THE INSPIRING I

- Stay undistracted when others are speaking to you. Avoid interrupting. Talk less, listen more.
- Be content with routine. Not everyone enjoys your spontaneity.
- Slow your pace. Not everyone can think or move as quickly as you.
- Don't use persuasion and charm to get your own way.
- Be consistent about returning things to their proper place.
- Guard against compromising your principles to gain acceptance and approval.
- Develop a system for remembering appointments, birthdays, anniversaries, and other important dates.
- Fulfill your commitments, even if something more fun comes along.

MODIFICATIONS FOR THE STEADY S

- Be more open to change. Things don't always go as planned.
- Avoid comparing yourself with other personality styles.
- Work at expressing your feelings, thoughts, and opinions.
- Increase your pace to accomplish your goals.
- Remember that your security is in God, not in your job or people.
- Guard against feeling intimidated by the D and C task-oriented folks.
- Work through hurt feelings. Forgive instead of holding a grudge.
- Practice making decisions.

MODIFICATIONS FOR THE CONSCIENTIOUS C

- Keep away from criticizing yourself and others.
- Learn to think and to speak more positively.
- Avoid frowning and giving disapproving looks.
- Do not be hard on yourself: perfectionism leads to procrastination.
- Stop working on tasks long enough to give time to relationships.
- Be careful not to withhold affection when you are hurt.
- Do not measure your self-worth based upon your performance.
- Give lots of praise, acceptance, and approval to others.

STRENGTH DRIVEN PERSONALITY

Understand that everyone operates out of either the strength side or the weakness side of his God-given behavioral traits. For example, directive **D** personality is known to be bold. A weakness driven **D** could be harsh and uncaring in the way he relates.

74 THE HOME EXPERIENCE

Sanctuary of Love

Be careful not to overdo your strengths. Any strength used to extreme becomes a weakness. For example, the fun loving **I** may be a great storyteller. However, if his storytelling never gives others a chance to talk, then he has monopolized the conversations. What was once a strength has now become a weakness.

Ask God to show you any areas of your personality that are currently weakness dominated. Then, rely on His help to change those weakness areas into strengths. Place your faith in God to help you to mature into a strength-driven person.

ENCOURAGING OTHERS

Encourage your family by making positive statements that build them up. This is not manipulation, but ways to say, "I love you." Each personality style is edified when their strengths are noticed and celebrated by others. For example, the steady S style likes to be complimented and appreciated more in a one-on-one relationship. Do not shout compliments for all to hear. They like gratitude to be given privately. Then again, the inspiring I temperament enjoys attention and public praise.[3]

FOR THE D FAMILY MEMBER
- You are self-confident.
- You are direct and get right to the point.
- You like to be in charge.
- You like responsibility.
- You are very determined.
- You are self-motivated.
- You can make decisions quickly.
- You have the ability to organize the whole family.
- You like to know the bottom line.
- You meet new challenges head on.
- You can act boldly and courageously.
- You are refreshed by doing something physical.

FOR THE I FAMILY MEMBER
- You are cute and charming.
- You are fun to be with.
- You are full of energy.
- You tell great stories.
- You are very positive.

- You enjoy spontaneity.
- You love to be around people.
- You are friendly and outgoing.
- You are motivated by what is fun.
- You have the ability to express yourself well.
- You like to be active and moving.
- You are refreshed by being with people.

FOR THE S FAMILY MEMBER

- You are a very loyal person.
- You are a great listener.
- You are a peacemaker.
- You value your family.
- You do not rush into making a decision.
- You bring calmness to a stressful situation.
- You help others feel at ease with your easy going manner.
- You are able to see both sides of a situation.
- You are most comfortable when there are no new changes.
- You like things written down or explained step by step.
- You feel other people's pain and hurts.
- You refresh by having time to relax and do nothing.

FOR THE C FAMILY MEMBER

- You are very creative.
- You feel things deeply.
- You are a list keeper.
- You have high standards.
- You are a very detailed person.
- You are very precise and accurate.
- You like to do the job right or not at all.
- You like to know all the facts before making a decision.
- You have high standards of excellence in some areas.
- You enjoy one-on-one relationships rather than large parties.
- You are a serious person, but that doesn't mean you are not happy.
- You enjoy refueling by spending time alone.

---

1 LaHaye, Tim. Transformed Temperaments. Tyndale House Publishers, 1993, pp. 18-20.

2 The DISC model will be used to explain four basic categories of personality. This system was developed by Dr. William Moulton Marston.

3 Charles F. Boyd. Different Children, Different Needs. Sisters, Oregon: Multnomah Books, 1994, pp. 150-153.

"*Live in peace with each other.*"

1 Thessalonians 5:13b

YOUR HOME EXPERIENCE
STUDY GUIDE

Personality Dynamics

PURPOSE: To improve your relationships by understanding personality differences and making adjustments in the way you relate to others.

1. Based upon your knowledge of the DISC personality styles, how would you describe your personality?

_____

_____

2. After close examination of the DISC personality chart, how would you describe others in your home?

_____

_____

3. Explain how a personality strength taken to extreme can become a weakness. Can you think of a specific way that you can avoid this from happening in your own life?

_____

_____

MAKING MODIFICATIONS

Understanding personality differences is essential for healthy relationships. Learning this skill takes practice and patience. The Apostle Paul knew how to relate to many different cultures and people groups. He chose to modify his own behavior so that he could spread the gospel by building close relationships with others.

"To the Jews I became like a Jew, to win the Jews…to the weak I became weak, to win the weak. I have become all things to all men so that by all possible means I might save some."
I CORINTHIANS 9:19-22

(4) Think of the different personality styles in your own home. What are some adjustments you can make to improve your relationships when relating to:

    a. The Directive **D**

         _____

         _____

    b. The Inspiring **I**

         _____

         _____

    c. The Steady **S**

         _____

         _____

    d. The Creative **C**

         _____

         _____

OPPOSITES ATTRACT

Notice the chart below. Opposites often attract each other. Make it your goal to attract and not attack others in your family.

D	I
Faster paced Decisive Risk taking	Fun loving Spontaneous Active
C	**S**
Serious Scheduled Passive	Slower paced Indecisive Reserved

(5) Now that you have a better understanding of personality differences, what are some specific ways you can improve your relationships with family members who are opposite?

_____
_____
_____
_____
_____

ENCOURAGING WORDS

(6) Make it your practice to speak words that bring encouragement to those closest to you. Prayerfully review the encouraging phrases in this chapter for the four personality styles. Ask God to help you change your language from destructive to constructive speech.

What are some edifying words you can say to:
The Dynamic **D**s in your family?

_____
_____
_____

The Inspiring **I**s?

_____
_____
_____

The Steady **S**s?

_____
_____
_____

The Creative **C**s?

_____
_____
_____

"Therefore encourage one another and build each other up,
just as in fact you are doing."
I THESSALONIANS 5:11

"*My command is this: Love each*

other as I have loved you."

John 15:12

REDUCING FAMILY CONFLICTS

"Live in peace with each other."

I THESSALONIANS 5:13b

This chapter is designed to show you how to minimize conflicts by understanding the DISC personality styles. You will discover how each personality style refuels, how each handles sensitive issues, and what to do when conflicts arise.

HOW EACH PERSONALITY RECHARGES

It is important to understand and make room for the different ways that each behavioral style gets refreshed. You can promote peace in your home by helping each family member to recharge in a way that meets their individual needs. Start by becoming aware of these differences. What would be fun for the Inspiring **I** may be draining for the Cautious **C** personality style.

D Needs physical activity to recharge. This is particularly true if they have been sitting at a desk all day.

I Refuels by spending time with people. They are re-energized when they can interact with others.

S   Refuels by doing absolutely nothing. A great weekend for an **S** would be when there is nothing they have to do. They enjoy relaxing with a close friend with little or no activity.

C   Gets recharged by being alone. They may decide to use their creativity to work on a detailed project, listen to music, read, or simply relax.

IDENTIFYING PRESSURE POINTS

Following is a description of the four basic fears associated with the personality styles. Ask yourself this question: Are there certain things that will immediately irritate me or send my emotions soaring out of control? Have you ever observed this kind of behavior in your spouse or other family members?

Next is a description of the fear associated with each personality style. Once you recognize these vulnerable areas, you can better deal with conflict situations.

THE DIRECTIVE D
Fears being taken advantage of.

The task-oriented **D** loves to lead and is focused on getting the job done. He feels good when others carry their share of the load. When the **D** feels that he has been left with your responsibilities as well as his own, he feels taken advantage of. He will then try to take control of his environment by being forceful, more direct, and aggressive. His forceful behavior can be very intimidating to others.

THE INFLUENCING I
Fears being disliked or rejected.

The inspiring **I** wants you to like him. This personality type can become a people pleaser. In an attempt to win your favor the **I** may become more friendly, outgoing, talkative, or diplomatic. As children and teens they are very susceptible to pressure from their peers. Since this fear is unreasonable, the **I** may compromise values, ideas, or important decisions in order to please others. Also, if the **I** is in an environment where he does not feel accepted, he may become quiet and withdrawn.

THE STEADY S
Fears the loss of security and change.

Any kind of a change, big or small, can trigger this fear. A loss of security can result from something as simple as rearranging their bedroom furniture, or as drastic as losing a job or a loved one. The steady **S** likes a very predictable environment with little or no changes. The peace loving **S** may combat this fear by becoming more cautious, slow-paced, methodological, friendly, or submitting. During these times of insecurity and change the **S** finds it very difficult to make decisions. They will try to control their environment by slowing down and acting more cautious.

THE CREATIVE C
Fears criticism.

The cautious **C** fears being personally criticized or that their work or performance will come under attack. The **C** may withdraw or become defensive, detailed, or questioning. This temperament is very sensitive and can be easily hurt by a comment that was never intended to offend. The **C** takes prides in doing the job right. This tendency to want things absolutely correct—sometimes by self imposed standards—can drive them to perfectionism. This behavior can also lead to conflict in relationships as the **C** may attempt to impose unrealistic standards on others.

IDENTIFYING RESPONSES TO CONFLICT
Every healthy family unit deals with conflicts. The next illustration will help you to recognize how each personality style may respond when faced with tension and disagreement. This knowledge will help you guard against taking someone's reaction as a personal affront.[2]

INITIAL RESPONSE

D	**Aggressive**	Demanding, bold, challenging
I	**Aggressive**	Wordy, cute, sarcastic, loud
S	**Passive**	Conforming, withdrawn, calm
C	**Passive**	Moody, defensive, withdrawn

These initial responses coincide with each temperament. For example, the **D** and **I** styles are naturally outgoing and aggressive. The **S** and **C** styles are normally laid back and compliant. However, as tensions increase each temperament suppresses their natural inclination and acts contrary to their normal behaviors as shown below.

IF PRESSURE CONTINUES

D	**Passive**	Resigning, turns you off
I	**Passive**	Conforming, seeks approval
S	**Aggressive**	Attacking, angry
C	**Aggressive**	Demanding, exaggerated criticism

HELP FROM THE HOLY SPIRIT

Some people rarely ever reach this second level of response especially if they are Spirit controlled. *"So I say, live by the Spirit, and you will not gratify the desires of the sinful nature."* Gal. 5:16. To live your life by the Spirit means to walk in love. The Holy Spirit empowers us to live our lives controlled by love instead of fear.

The four personality styles can either compliment or clash with each other. When stressful situations are handled with love and gentleness, relationships are healed and restored. When loving choices are made to make adjustments and allowances, intimacy and peace can be restored. Make it your aim to live your life by the power of the Holy Spirit.

WAYS TO REDUCE CONFLICT

Here are some valuable tips that will help you to connect more easily with both adults and children.[3]

RELATING TO THE DECISIVE D

The **D** Adult

- Avoid power struggles over control.
- Don't lecture or nag.
- Keep away from a negative focus. They are results oriented and want solutions.
- Share in a clear, straightforward and concise manner.
- Understand that they are more interested in getting the job done, than perfection.
- Don't be intimidated when **D**s come at you.

The **D** Child

- Set clear limits and boundaries. Be direct and to the point.
- Don't argue with this quick thinking and decisive youngster.
- The **D** will frequently push the limits. Expect confrontation and remain calm.
- This strong-willed child needs to understand that you are in control. Do not be intimidated by his demands.
- Remember that this youngster desires instant action. Teach him patience. Do not give in to unreasonable demands.

❧ Make strong, brief statements and establish your authority.

❧ Don't set unreasonably high standards or be overly critical or this child may give up.

RELATING TO THE INTERACTIVE I

The **I** Adult

❧ Allow time for socialization and small talk.

❧ Say something positive about how they look or what they have done.

❧ Compliment them on their appearance, accomplishments, or verbal skills.

❧ Understand that they fear rejection or loss of social approval.

❧ Provide an atmosphere free of criticism so be liberal with praise and acceptance.

❧ Don't push them for perfection.

❧ Recognize that they love change, excitement, and variety.

The **I** Child

❧ Realize that this child has difficulty getting organized—their room, drawers, and desks may tend to be messy.

❧ Be aware of this conflict of interest: getting things done versus having fun.

❧ Do chores or projects with them and add some fun. The **I** is very relational.

❧ Listen enthusiastically to your child's long stories whenever possible.

❧ Give lots of affection, praise, and approval.

RELATING TO THE STEADY S

The **S** Adult

❧ Explain how you want things done, not expecting the **S** to figure out the details.

❧ Be open and share your feelings. They are highly relational.

❧ Don't violate their trust. They put lots of energy into trusting and being trustworthy.

❧ Avoid making too many changes. They thrive on repeated patterns.

❧ Know that they will try to regain control of the environment by slowing the pace.

❧ Express genuine love, appreciation, and affection, but not too much publicly.

❧ Slow your pace and be patient in drawing out their inner feelings.

The **S** Child

❧ Keep in mind that this child is slow to change and enjoys routine.

❧ Accept their shyness. Don't bring lavish attention to them in public. Give them praise in private.

❧ When possible, give advance warning of how things may change.

❧ Slow the pace. Remember that the **S** refuels by relaxing and doing nothing. This does not mean they are lazy.

🙚 Don't try to force this youngster to discuss his feelings. He will talk only when ready.

🙚 Encourage forgiveness since the **S** tends to hold on to grudges.

🙚 Patiently encourage this youngster to make decisions without your input.

RELATING TO THE CONSCIENTIOUS C

The **C** Adult

🙚 Slow your pace, allowing time for thinking and detailed processing.

🙚 Don't be critical. Remember that the **C** feels things very deeply.

🙚 Avoid springing things on them. They like a controlled, predictable environment.

🙚 Bear in mind that they require time alone or time to work on a project to refuel.

🙚 Avoid generalized statements like, "You always…" or "You never…" or the **C** may become very defensive.

🙚 Give details and factual data to help them process information.

🙚 Afford them adequate time, but provide a deadline for action or decision.

The **C** Child

🙚 Don't over react to criticisms spoken by a **C**. Gently guide the child into a healthy acceptance of the shortcomings of others.

🙚 This child is deliberate and needs time to think before making decisions.

🙚 Be patient, answering detailed questions to help process information and get the facts.

🙚 Correct gently, since the **C**'s greatest fear is criticism.

🙚 Recognize that the child likes working on a project and is detail oriented.

🙚 Train against self-criticism and perfectionism.

🙚 Remind the child of the positive things from his day. One negative incident can cause the **C** to feel that the whole day was horrible.

> *"Finally, all of you, live in harmony with one another:*
> *be sympathetic, love as brothers, be compassionate and humble.*
> *Do not repay evil with evil or insult with insult,*
> *but with blessing because to this you were called*
> *so that you may inherit a blessing."*
> I PETER 3:8-9

1 Kulkin, Sanford: Person to Person Certification Cassette Tape Series. New Castle, PA: The Institute for Motivational Living Inc., 1993.

2 Boyd, Charles F. and David Boehi. *Different Children Different Needs: The Art of Adjustable Parenting.* (OR: Multnomah Books, Sisters, 1994), p. 173.

3 Boyd, p. 116-131.

YOUR HOME EXPERIENCE
STUDY GUIDE

Reducing Family Conflicts

PURPOSE: To gain insight and understanding into how to promote peaceful relationships in your home.

SENSITIVITY TO OTHERS

Conflicts can be minimized by understanding what triggers an emotional response. Being sensitive to how each family member refuels will be a valuable tool in promoting peaceful relationships. This chapter identified specific ways that each personality style likes to be refreshed.

1 Review the DISC recharging methods. How do you like to recharge?

_____

_____

_____

_____

_____

2 Can you identify how each member of your family likes to recharge?

_____

_____

_____

_____

_____

3 Think of creative ways in which you can allow each member of your family to refuel when planning your weekend or next vacation. This is not an easy task.

_____

_____

_____

_____

_____

_____

FAMILY PRESSURE POINTS

④ As you have discovered there is a basic pressure point or fear associated with each personality style. Given the right circumstances, this weakness can rear its ugly head. Learning about these four basic fears can help you understand some tension filled moments in your home. What is your greatest fear? How have you dealt with this in your personal life?

_____
_____
_____

⑤ Greatest fear of the **D** is being taken _____ of.

⑥ Greatest fear of the **I** is rejection, loss of _____ approval.

⑦ Greatest fear of the **S** is change or loss of _____.

⑧ Greatest fear of the **C** is criticism of _____ or
_____.

⑨ Prayerfully ask God to give you ways of relating to others in your family that will avoid provoking these fearful responses. Record your thoughts here.

_____
_____
_____
_____

⑩ What are some ways that you can help your children to live strength-driven lives so that these weaknesses do not control them during tense situations?

_____
_____
_____
_____
_____

⑪ Can you remember the initial responses to conflict mentioned in this chapter?

D = _____

I = _____

S = _____

C = _____

⑫ If tension persists how does the behavior of each personality change?

D = _____

I = _____

S = _____

C = _____

⑬ When we partner with the Holy Spirit and allow Him to change us, we react less and choose our responses more carefully. The most loving response to conflict is to adjust our own reactions. Here are some ways to adjust your response when dealing with each personality. Can you add more?

The Dynamic **D**

❧ Slow your pace.

❧ Practice patience.

❧ _____

❧ _____

The Inspiring **I**

❧ Listen more and talk less.

❧ Control emotional responses.

❧ _____

❧ _____

The Steady **S**

❧ Be more open to change.

❧ Be willing to confront.

❧ _____

❧ _____

The Creative **C**

❧ Avoid negative speaking.

❧ Accept yourself and others.

❧ _____

❧ _____

"Finally all of you, live in harmony,
be compassionate and humble.
Do not repay evil with evil or insult with insult,
but with blessing."

I PETER 3:8-9

"Do not let any unwholesome talk come out of your mouths, but only what is helpful for building others up according to their needs..."

~Ephesians 4:29

7 HONORING YOUR HUSBAND

"She comforts, encourages, and does him only good as long as there is life within her."

PROVERBS 31:12

Do not just have a good marriage, have an exceptional marriage. Learn what it means to honor your husband.

Being submissive to your mate is not necessarily the same thing as showing him honor. You can outwardly submit, but you cannot truly honor him unless your heart is right. Honor goes beyond submission because it requires that your thoughts, words, and actions line up.

WHAT DOES IT MEAN TO HONOR YOUR HUSBAND?

Webster defines honor as "high regard or respect; adherence to principles considered right; to respect greatly." Your husband seeks and needs honor, respect, praise, and encouragement from you.

"...let the wife see that she respects and reverences her husband
[that she notices him, regards him, honors him, prefers him,
venerates, and esteems him; and that she defers to him,
praises him, and loves and admires him exceedingly]."

EPHESIANS 5:33b AB

Honoring your spouse is a choice you make daily. Your emotions should not dictate your level of obedience. Although you may not always feel like it, you can make your mind up to show respect to your spouse in very practical ways. Make a good marriage great with these practical tips.

THOUGHTS, WORDS, AND ACTIONS

Honoring your husband involves the way you think of him, speak about him, and act toward him. Your thoughts shape your words. Your words direct your actions. Your actions govern your relationship. Honoring your spouse starts with two important ingredients— forgiveness and acceptance.

HONORING THOUGHTS OF...

...forgiveness

Forgive him for not being the leader, lover, listener, provider, friend, handyman, or whatever else you think he should be. Continually forgive as the Lord has forgiven you.

...acceptance

Your husband can sense when you accept him unconditionally. He can sense if you approve or disapprove of him by your attitude, body language, and lack of joy in his presence. With God's power you can provide an atmosphere of unconditional love and acceptance.

...reflection

Continually reflect on his strengths, not on his weaknesses. Always try to remember that it is not your job to correct him. I once thought that it was my God-given duty to help "fix" my husband. I have since learned that the Holy Spirit can do a much better and quicker job as you simply love him.

...restoration

Restore your relationship with your husband by breaking down emotional walls of hurt and hostility. He may have injured you deeply, but walls will seal rather than heal your wounds.

> *"Above all, love each other deeply,*
> *because love covers over a multitude of sins."*
> I PETER 4:8

...contentment

Learn to be content with your life partner. Don't compare him with other men or have unrealistic expectations. This, however, does not mean that you should be content to live in an abusive or potentially dangerous relationship. God does not want you to live in fear. Always seek help in these matters.

...respect

See your husband as God sees him—loved, forgiven, and valued as the one who carries the mantel of headship in your relationship. *"...and the wife must respect her husband."* Eph. 5:33b

...togetherness

You may want to emotionally pull away from him at times, thinking that he is undeserving of your love and affection. Don't give into these emotions. Honor him because, by doing so, you are honoring God through your obedience.

HONORING WORDS WHICH...

...build

Speak dozens of building words before ever speaking a word of rebuke. Refer to the list of honoring phrases that follows.

...encourage

Speak uplifting words about his strengths in the presence of others. Never point out his weaknesses or make jokes at his expense.

...heal

Be quick to say "I'm sorry" with no "buts" added. Then be patient as you allow your mate time and space for God to bring healing into the relationship.

...wait

Learn to press the pause button. When you are upset, regain control of your emotions and pray for wisdom before speaking.

...affirm

Be cautious about offering advice without an invitation to do so. In this way you will demonstrate confidence in his leadership.

...show respect

Your speech should always reflect an attitude of respect. The use of polite words such as: please, thank you, excuse me, and you are welcome.

...give grace

Allow your husband room to fail. Never say, "See, I told you so." or, "If only you would have listened to me."

...express patience

Remember to cast your cares on the Lord, not on your husband. Stop nagging him and learn to be quiet.

...agree

Listen without continually challenging his decisions. Remember that marriage is a partnership, not a competition.

...promote peace

Plan a convenient time to discuss important issues. Avoid talking about touchy subjects late at night when you are both tired.

...demonstrate unity

Let your children and others hear you speak honoring words about your husband.

EXAMPLES OF HONORING PHRASES

Ask the Lord to help you with positive statements that will honor your mate.

- You put God first in your life.
- You are a godly leader in our home.
- You control your anger rather than being controlled by it.
- You are especially strong in the area of _____.
- You treat others with respect.
- You are a faithful husband.
- You are a loving and wise father to our children.
- You make me feel secure.
- You don't tear down others to build yourself up.
- You are not intimidated by people more talented than you.
- You are a man of inner strength.
- You are fun to be with.
- I have complete confidence and trust in you.

HONORING ACTIONS THAT...

...meet HIS needs

Wives often mistakenly give to their husbands what they need rather than what he needs.
The Four **B**'s that husbands need.

- Backed (support, uplift, and encourage)
- Bedded (offer affection and sexual intimacy)
- Boarded (provide meals and a comfortable home)
- Babied (care for him when he is sick or feeling down)

The Four **L**'s that wives needs.

- Loved (both in words and actions)
- Lead (through kind direction and example)
- Lifted up (encouraged, romanced, made to feel special)
- Listened to (without trying to solve all her problems)

...promote peace

Body language can speak louder than words. A calm, peaceful countenance is a powerful statement during times of chaos.

...show interest

Be interested in what interests him. Find out what he would like you to do. You were created to be his helpmate. He was not created to be yours.

...say I love you!

Write him special love notes mentioning qualities you admire. Post them on the steering wheel of his car, the bathroom mirror, or other places to surprise him.

...demonstrate desire

Nothing is more attractive to your mate than to know that you desire him.

...show concern

Be sensitive when he has had a difficult day. Give him a night off by putting away your list of "to do's."

...feed him

Set an attractive table serving some of his favorite foods. Do not wait for a special occasion. Prepare meals that he likes and not always what your children like.

...give him space

Don't unload on him about how difficult your day was the moment he enters the house. Give him some time to relax and unwind.

...welcome

Greet him at the door when he arrives home with a smile, a hug, and a kiss.

...serve

Many times we serve our children and train our husbands. Instead, we should be serving our husbands and training our children.

...let go

Wives sometimes feel that it is their duty to fix their husband. God can do in six minutes what you haven't been able to accomplish in six years.

...don't mother him

Mothering is smothering. This nurturing position works great with children, but not with your spouse.

...create romance

Surprise him with a special evening at home. Be affectionate, hold hands, and put your arms around him. Light a candle, attractively arrange fruit, cheese and crackers on a tray, and spend time together.

...involve the children

Teach your children to joyfully serve their dad. This helps to prepare daughters to do the same for their husbands. It also influences sons to seek a wife who is willing to honor him by serving.

...promote growth

Allow him space to grow up. If he fails at something, do not step in and try to bail him out of his responsibilities.

LOVE VS. FEAR

Honor means to put love, not fear, into practice. Some women are afraid to submit to their husband's leadership. They are afraid to give up control and allow him to lead. What if he doesn't make the right decisions? Sarah, Abraham's wife, is our example of not giving way to fear. Decide to be like Sarah by letting go of your control and allowing God to work in your marriage.

> *"It was thus that Sarah obeyed Abraham*
> *[following his guidance and acknowledging his headship over her by]*
> *calling him lord (master, leader, authority).*
> *And you are now her true daughters if you do right*
> *and let nothing terrify you [not giving way to hysterical fears*
> *or letting anxieties unnerve you]."*
> I PETER 3:6 AB

COMMITMENT

Every marriage goes through testing and trials. As you draw close to God during the difficult years, the trials will help make, not break, your relationship. Choose right now to ride out the storms of life and stay together. As you honor your husband, God honors you.

> *"And that's about it, friends. Be cheerful. Keep things in*
> *good repair. Keep your spirits up. Think in harmony. Be agreeable*
> *Do all that, and the God of love and peace will be with you for sure.*
> II COR. 12:11 MSG

CHRIST-CENTERED MARRIAGE

As a believer in Christ you can choose to walk either the path of a Christ-centered lifestyle or the path of a self-centered lifestyle. The first path is constructive while the self-centered path is destructive.

A self-centered person makes everything about themselves. Statements are made like: "When do I get a break?"; "What about me?"; "What about my feelings?"; or "You don't care about me." This kind of attitude opens the door for self-pity. Self-pity results in anger, hurt, and resentment which make honoring your mate increasingly difficult.

Please understand that anyone entering marriage with unhealthy expectations will not find these needs being met. For example, a lonely person who marries to rid themselves of loneliness will still be lonely after years of marriage. Why? Because loneliness is a void that only God can fill. Once you purpose in your heart to live a Christ-centered life, He will meet your deepest needs.

A HUSBAND WHO DISOBEYS GOD

The following scripture applies to all men—those who are Christians and those who are not. It addresses a husband who is not obeying the Word of God. Notice that the passage specifically tells wives what to do. Don't talk! Keep quiet and let your partner be won over by your quiet, reverent, submissive, tender, calm, and loving behavior.

> *"In like manner, you married women, be submissive*
> *to your own husbands [subordinate yourselves*
> *as being secondary to and dependent on them,*
> *adapt yourselves to them], so that*
> *even if any do not obey the Word [of God],*
> *they may be won over not by discussion*
> *but by the [godly] lives of their wives."*
> I PETER 3:1 AB

JUST DO IT!

My friend's husband once said, "Will you please stop telling me how you are going to change. Just do it." I encourage you not to make promises to your spouse about how you are going to change. Instead, depend upon God to help you make wise decisions about your thoughts, words, and actions. Then watch as God transforms your marriage.

YOUR HOME EXPERIENCE
STUDY GUIDE

Honoring Your Husband

PURPOSE: To discover how to honor your husband with a pure heart and loving actions.

A NOTE TO SINGLE GALS

You may wonder why you are even turning to this page right now. After all, you are not married. You may have had a husband at one time. Perhaps you have never been married. Whatever the reason, you are now single. Regardless of your current status, your situation may change. I believe that if you have a strong godly desire to be married, then God has someone for you. Why not use this time to get into shape while waiting for God to bring your mate into your life?

Think of this section as training for developing skills useful in building a strong future marriage. Do not wait until you are married. Begin now. Ask God to show you how you can prepare for your tomorrows. Even if marriage is not a desire of yours, please consider reading this anyway. This information can be useful to you in understanding and encouraging others who are married.

WHAT DOES IT MEAN TO HONOR YOUR HUSBAND?

1 The most loyal wife can appear to be very submissive to her husband and yet not honor him. How can this happen?

_____

_____

_____

2 What does it mean to honor your husband? After reading Ephesians 5:22 please restate this verse in your own words. *"...let the wife see that she respects and reverences her husband [that she notices him, regards him, honors him, prefers him, venerates, and esteems him; and that she defers to him, praises him, and loves and admires him exceedingly]."* Ephesians 5:33b AB

_____

_____

_____

③ There are times when I honestly do not "feel" like honoring my husband. Read the scripture passage which states: "Wives, submit to your husbands as to the Lord." (Ephesians 5:22) What does this verse mean to you?

_____

_____

_____

_____

_____

_____

HONORING THOUGHTS

④ Consider the thoughts that go through your mind each day concerning your husband. Are they constructive or destructive? Like many wives, you may need to do some mental house cleaning. The Scriptures call this renewing your mind. Consider the following mentally healthy exercise. Whenever negative thoughts enter your mind about your husband, replace these thoughts with positive ones.

Write down honoring thoughts about your mate concerning:

Forgiveness: _____

Acceptance: _____

Restoration: _____

Contentment: _____

Respect: _____

HONORING WORDS

⑤ Our words are vitally important to building a healthy marriage. Jesus said, *"For out of the overflow of the heart the mouth speaks."* Matthew 12:34b. Think of the way that you speak to your spouse. What destructive words do you need to lose? What constructive words do you need to choose? Consider the following exercise. Write down words and phrases you can say that will:

Build the relationship: _____

Bring encouragement: _____

Promote healing: _____

Demonstrate greater respect: _____

Bring greater unity: _____

HONORING ACTIONS

⑥ Please read the Four "B's" that husbands need as noted in the book. Then read the Four L's that women need. Ask yourself this question: "Have I given to my husband what he needs, or have I given him what I need?" What are some major differences you notice about the needs of husbands and wives?

_____
_____
_____
_____
_____
_____
_____

⑦ How can you show that you love, cherish, and respect your mate? Every man is different in what he would like you to do. If you do not "feel" love or respect, show it anyway. Be obedient to the Word of God and show honor to your husband as "unto the Lord." As you love and respect him, you are obeying God's commands. This pleases the Lord and He will reward you for your obedience. If you wait for your feelings to catch up to what your mind knows you are to do, you may never begin.

_____
_____
_____
_____
_____
_____
_____

⑧ Write down your plan of action. You may want to look at the suggestions in the book to give you some fresh ideas. Have fun with this. Be creative!

_____
_____
_____
_____
_____
_____
_____
_____

The illustration of Sarah's obedience to her husband, Abraham, is a powerful example of never giving place to fear. A wife who feels that she must be in control all of the time is living out of fear. She is afraid to let go and trust God. Obedience to the Word of God will bring healing to one's need to always be in control. Read the scripture below and consider following Sarah's example.

"It was thus that Sarah obeyed Abraham
[following his guidance and acknowledging his headship over her by]
calling him lord (master, leader, authority).
And you are now her true daughters if you do right
and let nothing terrify you [not giving way to hysterical fears
or letting anxieties unnerve you]."
I PETER 3:6 AB

⑨ In what way can this Scripture be practically applied to your life today?

_____
_____
_____
_____

⑩ Spend time in prayer for your husband. Let your mind dwell on those things about him that you are most thankful for. Then, begin to intercede on your husband's behalf by asking God to bless his life. Be specific. Also, be honest with God. If there is an area of your relationship that you are having trouble with, bring this concern before the Lord. Nothing is too small or even too big for Him.

_____
_____
_____
_____

Meditate on this Scripture:

"Do not be anxious about anything,
but in everything, by prayer and petition,
with thanksgiving, present your requests to God.
And the peace of God, which transcends all understanding,
will guard your hearts and your minds in Christ Jesus."
PHILIPPIANS 4:6-7

"May the Lord make

and overflow for each

your love increase

other...."

~ 1 Thessalonians 3:12

Haven o

HOME ORDER

f Peace

HOME LIFESTYLE

HOME ORDER

8

PRIORITY MANAGEMENT—A VALUE OF ORDER
Priority Management—A Value of Order Study Guide

9

HOME ORGANIZATION—A VALUE OF PEACE

10

CLEANING—A VALUE OF GRATITUDE

PRIORITY MANAGEMENT —A VALUE OF ORDER

*"Teach us to number our days aright,
that we may gain a heart of wisdom."*

PSALMS 90:12

Discover ways to sensibly manage all areas of your life. By prioritizing according to God's principles, you can learn what it means when Jesus said, *"My yoke is easy and my burden is light."* You will learn how to live the abundant life that God intended as you manage your priorities.

Time Management is a term that most of us have heard. I believe that there is no such thing as time management, only self-management. Each of us must manage our activities during the 24-hour time frame ordained by God. On the other hand, priority management is a biblical concept.

Prioritize means "to put in order of importance". This is no different for women today than it was for women during Bible times. The Scriptures are applicable to every generation in every circumstance. If you desire to live a life pleasing to God, it is critical that you make intelligent choices based on God's priorities.

"Look carefully then how you walk!
Live purposefully and worthily and accurately,
not as unwise and witless, but as wise (sensible, intelligent people),
making the very most of the time (buying up each opportunity)
because the days are evil."

EPHESIANS 5:15-16

HERE'S THE PLAN

I believe that Proverbs 31:10-31 is God's priority plan for women. The "woman of noble character" is a strong model for all women who desire to live a godly lifestyle. She was a wise planner, a supportive wife, the keeper of her home, a nurturing mother, a prudent manager, a skilled business woman, a counselor, an aide to the needy, and much more. She gracefully carried out all these roles with great kindness and joy.

A closer look at Proverbs 31 will give incredible insight. These are the words of "Lemuel king of Massa, which his mother taught him." Many scholars believe that King Lemuel was Solomon whose mother was Bathsheba.

10 A wife of noble character who can find? She is worth far more than rubies.

11 Her husband has full confidence in her and lacks nothing of value.

12 She brings him good, not harm, all the days of her life.

13 She selects wool and flax and works with eager hands.

14 She is like the merchant ships, bringing her food from afar.

15 She gets up while it is still dark; she provides food for her family
and portions for her servant girls.

16 She considers a field and buys it; out of her earnings she plants a vineyard.

17 She sets about her work vigorously; her arms are strong for her tasks.

18 She sees that her trading is profitable, and her lamp does not go out at night.

19 In her hand she holds the distaff and grasps the spindle with her fingers.

20 She opens her arms to the poor and extends her hands to the needy.

21 When it snows, she has no fear for her household; for all of them are clothed in scarlet.

22 She makes coverings for her bed; she is clothed in fine linen and purple.

23 Her husband is respected at the city gate, where he takes his seat
among the elders of the land.

24 She makes linen garments and sells them, and supplies the merchants with sashes.

25 She is clothed with strength and dignity; she can laugh at the days to come.

26 She speaks with wisdom, and faithful instruction is on her tongue.

27 She watches over the affairs of her household and does not eat the bread of idleness.

28 Her children arise and call her blessed; her husband also, and he praises her:

29 "Many women do noble things, but you surpass them all."

30 Charm is deceptive, and beauty is fleeting; but a woman who fears the LORD is to be praised.

31 Give her the reward she has earned, and let her works bring her praise at the city gate.

PROVERBS 31:10-31

For many years I steered away from reading this passage. I thought to myself, "Why even bother reading these verses?" You will never measure up to this superwoman. The truth is that I did not understand how her life was so fruitful until the Lord gave me insight into this incredible passage.

How did the Proverbs woman accomplish so much and still be able to laugh at the days to come? She had her priorities straight. Let us take a closer look at each of the priorities as they relate to the scriptures.

PRIORITY 1: THE FEAR OF THE LORD

Without a respectful fear of the Lord, a woman can become self-occupied, preoccupied, or unoccupied—all of which are destructive.

The woman of Proverbs 31 did not just wake up one day and find herself a woman of noble character with a husband and children who lavish praise on her. This lifestyle was something she grew into because of her reverence of the Lord (Proverbs 31:30). She demonstrated that her first priority was God by the fact that she feared Him enough to obey Him.

What are the benefits of having a healthy fear of the Lord?

❧ Wisdom   *"The fear of the Lord is the beginning of wisdom...."*
                   Psalms 111:10

                   Wisdom means to have insight beyond the capability of your mind. God gives us wisdom by revelation.

❧ Knowledge   *"The fear of the Lord is the beginning of knowledge...."*
                   Proverbs 1:7

                   God not only gives knowledge to those who fear Him, but

also gives understanding of how to make use of it.

❧ Length to Life	*"The fear of the Lord adds length to life…."*	Proverbs 10:27

❧ Protection and Deliverance	*"The angel of the Lord encamps around those who fear him and he delivers them."*	Psalm 34:7

❧ Family Security and Refuge	*"He who fears the Lord has a secure fortress, and for his children it will be a refuge."*	Proverbs l4:26

❧ Fountain of Life	*"The fear of the Lord is a fountain of life…."*	Proverbs 14:27

PRIORITY 2: HER HUSBAND…IF SHE IS MARRIED

The married woman's second priority is her husband. This requires a commitment to obey God by loving her husband in practical ways. .

> *"…a married woman is concerned about the affairs of this world*
> *—how she can please her husband."*
>
> I CORINTHIANS 7:34b

- ❧ Her primary call is to be a *"helper meet (suitable, adapted, and complimentary) for him."* (Genesis 2:20 AB)
- ❧ Because of her willingness to serve him, he lacks nothing of value. (Proverbs 31:11)
- ❧ He has full confidence in her because she is trustworthy, honorable, edifying and always kind. (Proverbs 31:11, 29)
- ❧ She is not interested in tearing him down, but rather, in building him up.
- ❧ She thinks of his needs before her own.
- ❧ She brings him good, not harm, all the days of her life. (Proverbs 31:12)
- ❧ She is praised by her husband. (Proverbs 31:28)

Spending focused time with your children is important. Keep in mind, how-ever, that it is God's will that the husband and wife spend more time bond-ing with each other than with the children. A marriage that orbits around the children rather than the parents will eventually spin out of control. The benefits of a marriage-centered family are as great for the children as for the parents. And when the children are gone from the home, the marriage relationship will not be disrupted but will continue to grow in intimacy and unity.

LARRY TITUS, PRESIDENT OF KINGDOM GLOBAL MINISTRIES

HER LORD…IF SHE IS UNMARRIED

"An unmarried woman or virgin is concerned about the Lord's affairs: Her aim is to be devoted to the Lord in both body and spirit."

I CORINTHIANS 7:34a

The unmarried woman is to be devoted to the Lord. This requires a commitment to obey God in both body and spirit. The Lord wants to be involved in every aspect of the single woman's affairs.

Some of you who are reading this are single and satisfied. Others long to be married. I believe that if you have the desire to be married that God has a husband for you. While you are waiting for God to lead you into marriage, begin preparing by submitting to the Lord in every way.

- See yourself as married to Jesus.
- Before making decisions big or small consult with your "rich Jewish husband".
- Put your trust in the Lord to lead, provide for, and protect you.
- While you sit at your table, realize that you are never alone. The Lord is present with you at your table.

PRIORITY 3: HER HOME

Let me ask you this question. What were you given first to care for, a home or children? Most of you would say an apartment or a home. Don't make the common mistake of always putting activities with your children above caring for your home. Please work for a proper balance in these areas.

Never feel guilty about cleaning and caring for your home. Children will learn a healthy work ethic as they observe you taking good care of your possessions.

❧ She orders the affairs of her home which creates a peaceful environment. (Proverbs 31:15, 21, 27)

❧ She cares for her home and those who live there. (Proverbs 31:27)

❧ She is fully aware of all the activities that go on in her household. (Proverbs 31:27)

❧ She wisely purchases food, supplies, and whatever else is needed. (Proverbs 31:18)

❧ She takes advantage of sales and does not buy on impulse. (Proverbs 31:14)

❧ She does not feel guilty about doing housework before playing with children. (Proverbs 31:17, 19)

❧ She works diligently at making her home beautiful and comfortable. (Proverbs 31:13, 17, 22)

❧ She does not try to do everything herself, but assigns age appropriate household duties to children or enlists help from others. (Proverbs 31:15 AB)

❧ Because of her wise money management, smart shopping, and budgeting she is able to make wise financial decisions. (Proverbs 31:16, 18)

❧ She understands that she is serving God by managing her home affairs well. (Proverbs 31:30)

PRIORITY 4: HER CHILDREN

❧ Her children are well cared for. They have clothing, food, and other provisions. (Proverbs 31:15, 21)

❧ She teaches her children to submit to authority by her own example.

❧ She raises her children with discipline and the fear of the Lord. (Proverbs 31:30)

❧ She maintains a daily routine and assigns tasks for those in her home. (Proverbs 31:15 AB)

❧ She teaches her children the value of working, not only by her example, but also by requiring them to work at home and not just play. Instilling a strong work ethic at a young age will help them as teens and young adults make a successful transition into the World of Work. (Proverbs 31:15)

❧ She does not focus all her time and energy on her children's desires. Therefore her children are not self-centered and selfish. (Proverbs 31:16, 19, 20, 24)

❧ Because she works at keeping her priorities straight, her offspring live in a secure environment.

❧ She makes wise decisions by managing the activities of her young. (Proverbs 31:27)

❧ She trains her children by example to serve and respect their father. (Proverbs 31:12)

❧ She maintains self-control and wisdom is on her tongue when disciplining her children. (Proverbs 31:26)

PRIORITY 5: HER PRIVATE LIFE

- She does not neglect to care for her own personal needs. She takes time to rest, excercise, and renew her mind. She "girds herself with strength." (Proverbs 31:17)
- Even during times of hardship she keeps her eyes fixed on God who is the light in her life. *"…her lamp goes not out, but it burns on continually through the night [of trouble, privation, or sorrow, warning away fear, doubt, and distrust]."* (Proverbs 31:18 AB) I believe that *"her lamp"* represents the light that the Lord provides for those who will trust Him through difficulties.
- She speaks with wisdom revealing her knowledge of God. (Proverbs 31:26)
- She does not struggle with low self-esteem. She is complete in her calling. (Proverbs 31:25)
- She exhibits noble (excellent) character. She works at improving these traits. (Proverbs 31:10, 29)
- She maintains a pleasant attitude about her duties. (Proverbs 31:25)
- She is internally motivated and is not given to laziness. (Proverbs 31:27)
- She clothes herself to look attractive. Her clothing is of fine quality (Proverbs 31:22). I believe that she knows how to shop for bargains!
- She is not anxious. She purposes in her mind to laugh at the days to come. (Proverbs 31:25)

PRIORITY 6: HER PUBLIC LIFE

Her final priority includes activities outside of her home.

- She extends help to those who are in need of physical, emotional, or spiritual support. (Proverbs 31:20 AB)
- Her job, career, or even church involvement does not take priority over the other five areas mentioned.
- She has learned to say "No" when necessary. She only gets involved with what God has shown her to do.
- Her obedience in prioritizing her life (areas 1-5) position her for God's anointing to serve in the church and other public arenas. (Proverbs 31:31)
- She is wise in her business dealings. She does not overspend or buy impulsively. (verse 16)
- She uses her God-given gifts and talents creatively. This woman created and sold garments and sashes for profit. (Proverbs 31:19, 24)
- She is not swayed from her life call. She remains focused on God rather than on the fleeting pleasures of this world. (Proverbs 31:30)
- She has no desire to conform her life to the standards of the day, but lives by the principles set down in the Bible. (Proverbs 31:10, 31)

HOW TO BEGIN PRIORITIZING
PRAY

Prayerfully consider how these six priorities apply to your life. Since God is the only one with the blue print, He will be the only one to fill in the blanks of your unique situation.

RECORD

Record all of your activities during a normal day. Be sure to write down everything including: idle time, talking on the phone, watching TV, computer time, and sleeping. Then categorize each activity according to the six priorities above. By doing this you will become more conscious of what takes your time. Look for imbalances.

LIST

What on your list needs to be eliminated? Ask God for wisdom. Subtract from your list before adding to it. Learn to say "no." Remember, you are not God's gift to everyone, but you are God's gift to someone. Determine to limit your work to what you can handle. Busyness is not a virtue, but fruitfulness is.

ASK YOURSELF THE FOLLOWING QUESTIONS

- What needs to be added to or subtracted from my activities to accomplish the purpose for which I was born?
- What unhealthy habits need to be corrected in the way I think, act, and respond?
- Have I included daily time with God, who is my power source?

Whether single, married, widowed, or divorced you can see why it is so important for you to prioritize your life. Don't miss your part in the incredible master plan of God. Make it your choice to put into practice what you have heard. Then His power, love, and blessings will flow through your life. The choice is yours.

> *"Come to Me, all you who are weary*
> *and burdened, and I will give you rest.*
> *Take my yoke upon you and learn from me,*
> *for I am gentle and humble in heart,*
> *and you shall find rest for your souls."*
> MATTHEW 11:28-29

YOUR HOME EXPERIENCE
STUDY GUIDE

Priority Management

PURPOSE: To discover practical ways of putting your life in order.

Our focus will be on helping you to make the most of each day by living purposefully, sensibly, and intelligently. Please refer to Proverbs 31:10-31 as the foundation for this section.

PRIORITY 1: THE FEAR OF THE LORD

① What does it mean to have a healthy fear of the Lord?

_____

_____

② What are some of the benefits of fearing the Lord for you as well as for your family?

_____

_____

PRIORITY 2: HER HUSBAND...IF SHE IS MARRIED

③ What are some key scripture verses that substantiate this second priority in a woman's life?

_____

_____

④ If you are married, is your husband your second priority? If not, what adjustments do you feel need to be made?

_____

_____

HER LORD...IF SHE IS UNMARRIED

> *"An unmarried woman or virgin is concerned about the Lord's affairs:*
> *Her aim is to be devoted to the Lord in both body and spirit."*
>
> I CORINTHIANS 7:34a

⑤ As a single woman who is concerned about the Lord's affairs, is pleasing the Lord your second priority? What do you think it means "to be devoted to the Lord in both body and spirit"?

_____

_____

⑥ Give two practical examples of how you can make your "rich Jewish husband" your second priority.

_____

_____

PRIORITY 3: HER HOME

⑦ Why is it important to make your home the third highest priority? How will this precedent improve the quality of life for both you and your family?

_____

_____

⑧ Explain how ordering the affairs of your household can promote a peaceful environment. Please give some examples.

_____

_____

PRIORITY 4: HER CHILDREN

⑨ As a parent, you are responsible to love, discipline, and train your children so that they can become responsible adults. Is there a specific area of your relationship with your child (children) that has been neglected? If so, write it down. Ask God for wisdom concerning how to make the necessary changes.

_____

_____

⑩ What do you feel are the two the most important areas for you to concentrate on concerning your child's growth and character development?

_____

_____

PRIORITY 5: HER PRIVATE LIFE

Mothers of young children, working single moms, and many other women—both young and old—have neglected this aspect of their lives. Regardless of how busy you are right now, please try to find time—even if it is just for 15 minutes a day—to care for your personal needs. This includes your body, mind, and spirit. Without making deposits back into your life, you will have a tendency to burn out.

(11) List one area of your private life that you feel has been neglected recently. How can you creatively make the necessary changes?

_____

_____

(12) If you were to ask God what one thing He would like you to change regarding your personal life, what do you think He would say to you?

_____

_____

_____

PRIORITY 6: HER PUBLIC LIFE

Your public life represents everything you do outside of your home. This includes work, recreation, shopping, church, extended family and friends, volunteer work, errands, and all other activities.

(13) How would you describe your public life? Do you feel you need to make any adjustments here? If so, what are they?

_____

_____

_____

(14) The woman of Proverbs 31 had a very active and successful public life. She was praised in the city gates because of all that she stood for and accomplished both at home and in public. What would her life be like if her priorities were not in order? What advice would you give?

_____

_____

_____

"She watches over the affairs
of her household and does not eat
the bread of idleness."

Proverbs 31:27

HOME ORGANIZATION—
A VALUE OF PEACE

"But everything should be done in a fitting and orderly way."

I CORINTHIANS 14:40

An organized home gives a family security and peace. Without confusion and frenzy each family member can find what they need without bothering each other in a panic searching for their needed item. "Everything has a place and everything in its place" is an old adage that few find important enough to implement.

Creating order in your home is establishing a principle that has been proven from the beginning of time. Without order, there is chaos. In chaos, there is no peace. Without peace one cannot rest and renew energy.

It takes focus, time, and work to organize an unorganized home. However, the initial investment of time will pay in dividends of more relaxed free time to enjoy your relationships. Disorder consumes time in the same way paying interest consumes profits.

It is not my intention to provide you with a comprehensive book on organization. I want to simplify the process of organizing your home with short-cut ideas for each room in your house. By reading my ideas and creating your own, you can become inspired to apply what you already know is important.

GENERAL RULES FOR YOUR HOME ORGANIZATION PROCESS

1. Organize one room at a time.
2. Maintain the order of that room for at least one week before organizing another room.
3. Instruct your family on the new order of that room. Show them where things are located as if they have never been there before. Make your children feel like an important part of the team in managing the order of your home together. If necessary, instruct them on how to put things away and where to put them. Make it fun.
4. Prepare to re-organize by collecting the appropriate supplies.
5. Divide a big job into small sections.

Use three bags, boxes, or laundry baskets and label them *Give Away, Throw Away, Put Away.* I like to use a box for give away and a bag for throw away. I prefer to use a laundry basket for put away so I can see the items and easily carry them from room to room. Also, a box in your garage labeled "garage sale" helps you to be generous as you rid yourself of those precious things that you never use.

Schedule a time to begin. Move quickly. Run a race with yourself. Set your timer and see what you can accomplish in 30-minute segments. You will be surprised!

SUPPLIES YOU WILL NEED
ORGANIZE IT BY CONTAINING IT IS DEVI'S MOTTO

- Plastic trash bags
- Boxes
- Baskets
- Pail of water and cloth
- File folders
- Notebooks
- Markers and labels
- Turn tables
- Drawer Organizers
- Ziploc bags
- Small containers; shoe boxes or small plastic bins, etc.
- Hand-held broom or dust-buster
- Feather duster or wool duster

Keep your supplies in one place while you are on your reorganization mission. Contain them in a box or basket so you can easily move them from room to room. You will also want to store them together until you complete your project.

Reorganization must be done in increments and your supplies should be readily accessible to you during this process.

LET'S BEGIN ROOM BY ROOM
FRONT ENTRY

Your entrance is your "welcoming" center for everyone who enters. A clutter-free, colorful entry will make your family and friends want to stay. You should be able to accommodate coats, book-bags, boots, shoes, and mail with ease from your front entry. Whether your family takes their things to another room or stores them nearby, they should know exactly what to do with their "stuff" when they enter the door. Your guests will want to stay if you have prepared a place for them to be comfortable.

Consider the following tips for your entry.

- If closet space is limited and you have room for a wardrobe cabinet in your foyer, this works perfectly for children's backpacks, shoes, and jackets.

- Only larger homes have front entrance foyers and they are usually furnished for receiving guests. In this case the only organization needed is to prepare the coat closet to be used and viewed by guests.

- The closet nearest the front door should be used for the frequently worn coats. Most homes have limited storage space; therefore, seldom does one have the luxury of a "guest closet only." On the above shelf, in the closet, provide bins or nicely covered boxes for gloves, scarves, and hats. Also provide a set of stacked bins on one side of the closet for children's gloves and hats.

- If children use this closet, provide hooks, positioned at a comfortable height, for their coats.

- Leave room for a few heavyweight hangers for guest coats.

- Everything not hanging should be in a container.

- If you need a place for boots, provide a container for the boots. Do not just put them on the floor. They will always be in a heap.

- Ceramic decorative containers (usually used for plants) are great to use to sort your mail. Hang them in your foyer. One for your husband, one for the teenagers, and one for yourself.

❧ Sort the mail as you bring it indoors.

- Your husband will take his to the office (if he pays the bills).
- Put the remainder of the mail in your container and sort mail later at your "home information center." That is the place where you keep your daily calendar and important paperwork.
- Immediately throw away advertising mail that you do not want.
- Do not lay your mail on the foyer table or the kitchen counter.

LIVING/FAMILY ROOM

The living/family room is the place where you live. This multi-task room is vulnerable to chaos. Multi-faceted activities such as reading books, magazines, and newspapers, watching television, doing homework, eating refreshments, enjoying conversations, and taking cozy naps are all part of life in the family room. Lots of clutter can accumulate. Following are some ideas to help you maintain an orderly and warm environment.

❧ Contain your current magazines in a basket beside your chair. Tear out articles and file the ones you want to keep. Keep your "to be filed" folder in your basket so you can tear as you read. Discard the magazines and catalogues that you have read.

❧ Nap blankets should be part of your décor. Drape them across the arm of the sofa or chairs for easy use and easy put away.

❧ Store a nap pillow under the sofa, behind a chair or in an enclosed side console table. Trunks or chests make good coffee tables and are excellent storage for your cozy pillows and blankets. This also extends the life of your decorative pillows.

❧ Use CD organizers that are decorative and have easy access. If you have enclosed storage space, use a box or boxes and store by categories: vocal, instrumental, inspirational, worship, jazz, pop, classical, Christmas etc.

❧ Coasters should be part of the décor and easily accessible at all sitting areas.

❧ Small napkins can be incorporated in your décor also, having them readily available at all times.

Hide a lighter or matches in your magazine basket for your candles. Light a candle before you sit down. If you have young children look for another convenient safe place.

KITCHEN

The kitchen is one of the most used rooms in the home. Every family member does some kind of work in the kitchen—cooking, putting dishes away, setting the table, emptying the trash, or just "raiding the refrigerator." Therefore, organization is essential for efficiency in the kitchen.

When you organize your kitchen think *function, convenience,* and *space.* Consider how your kitchen is used most. Are you a baker? Do you prepare fresh food? Do you cook in a hurry? Your primary *function* will determine how you set up your kitchen. Some kitchens I have been in need to be completely reassigned. Something as simple as changing the storage place of your cooking utensils could give you new inspiration to cook and to prepare special times for your family from the kitchen. Remember: "…think *function, convenience,* and *space."*

FUNCTION

- Store items close to where they are used. Potholders should be near the stove and oven. Glasses near the sink or refrigerator, knives near your cutting area and so forth.

- My favorite way to store spices is in a drawer. I like to lay them on their side and line them up in alphabetical order. If you have both canned and jarred spices, use one side of the drawer for the cans and the other side for the jars.

- The double layer silverware drawer organizers are wonderful if they fit your drawers. If they do not, buy the individual module organizers and fit them according to your space.

- Store all flour and meal items in airtight containers to avoid infestation. Decorative canisters should only be used for frequently used items such as sugar. Packaged items like tea, sweeteners, or cocoa can be stored in the smaller ones.

- Similar items should be stored together. Baking goods, canned vegetables, canned fruits, canned soups, canned milk, cereals, dry foods (beans, pasta, rice) sauces, spreads, oils, vinegars, seasonings, etc.

- Under the sink. Because the space is tall, place an 8-gallon trash can to the right of your plumbing fittings. To the left, use a wire-coated shelf to store your dish detergent and cleaning agents. Slide a shallow dishpan under the shelf like a drawer. Store rubber gloves, sponges, and dishwasher brush in the dishpan. Put hooks on the inside of the door or on the side of the cabinet wall to hang a damp dishcloth. A tension rod mounted under the sink works great to dry damp towels and cloths.

🙠 Convert a deep drawer into a file cabinet for recipes, coupons, shopping ads or warranties. Cut file folders if necessary.

🙠 Create a message center. A chalkboard or white board with a cork section is ideal. Leave written messages for each other and pin up important reminders. Each family should check the message center when arriving home.

CONVENIENCE

🙠 A wire basket mounted under your top cabinet makes a great place for storing fresh fruit or potatoes and onions.

🙠 Place hooks everywhere. My measuring cups and spoons hang on hooks inside my baking cupboard.

🙠 Store your cooking spoons and spatulas in a decorative container near or on your stove. This will save you lots of digging time. Your choice is in front of you.

🙠 Use baskets or plastic containers inside your cupboards. Store your rice, beans, and bagged pasta in a basket. You can pull this out from a lower shelf as if it is a drawer. I do the same for baking goods. This eliminates the need to unload items in order to reach items in the back of the cabinet. Just pull out the basket and you can see everything.

🙠 If you have room, store each pot with its own lid. Lid racks mounted on inside cabinet doors help also. Store your pots and pans near the stove.

🙠 When loading the dishwasher, group your items together in the order that they are put away; forks, spoons, knives. If you use more than one style of flatware, sort them in the dishwasher.

🙠 Place several replacement trash bags in the bottom of your trashcans under the liner bag. When you remove the full one, you have a spare in the bottom to reline your can.

🙠 Turntables help to bring rear items to the front of the cupboard. They are great for canned goods. It is amazing how many cans you can stack and spin on a 12" turn table. Do not buy the multi-level turntables for canned goods. They are inefficient. They only work for short small items and tend to be unstable. Most cabinets do not have the height to accommodate the two-tier turntable. Turntables are also good for bottled items like soy sauce, vinegar, steak sauce, olive oil, etc.

SPACE

There are many innovative ways to find space in a crowded kitchen. Here are several suggestions.

- If your cabinetry is small you can mount exterior shelves and stack canned goods of like kind arranged with a small ivy plant.

- Potatoes and onions can be displayed in a basket.

- Make use of wire coated shelf racks for maximizing the use of your space. These work well in some cases for dishes.

- The backs of cupboard doors make good storage space. Watch for appropriate racks to attach. I have an organizer for my foil, plastic wrap and Ziploc bags mounted inside a door.

- Clear your counter spaces and make them pretty. Store seldom used appliances in the cupboard.

- A cutting board that fits across the sink expands your work counter area. I store my cutting boards under the sink standing along the wall.

- Use your wall spaces for hanging things to save counter and cupboard space. The microwave, hand mixer, can opener, and even the coffee maker can be mounted.

- Pots and pans can also be hung on the wall or on a rack suspended from the ceiling.

- I converted a hall closet just outside my kitchen to a pantry using a door mounted wire coated rack. I placed a ready-made shelf unit inside.

ORGANIZE THE REFRIGERATOR

- Refrigerators need to be cleaned out and wiped down regularly. The best time to do this is when you are low on food. I clean and reorganize my refrigerator every other week as I am putting away my groceries from my bimonthly shopping trip.

- Your freezer section also needs to be evaluated. Check dates. Remember freezing just slows spoilage—it does not prevent it.

- After throwing away old items, wash shelves and sides of the refrigerator. Don't forget the door. Also, wash meat and vegetable drawers.

❦ Line your vegetable drawer with a double layer of paper towels. This helps to absorb moisture from your washed vegetables.

❦ Group the items in your refrigerator and designate the shelves. Using my "store it by containing it" method, group items in containers. On top of my vegetable drawer I place a flat basket to hold additional fresh vegetables that do not fit in the drawer. I can pull this basket out as if it is a drawer.

❦ Use container trays for cheese, yogurt, mayonnaise and small dairy products; whipping cream, half-n-half, etc. My daughter uses a flat plastic tray with 2-inch sides. I use a small-scale cleaning caddy. It is divided and has a handle. I can lift the whole container to my counter if I am using several items. Or I can pull it out like a drawer to see what I have. I also use this drawer idea for jarred items; pickles, condiments, jams, etc.

❦ The use of vinyl placemats on the glass shelves makes the inside of your refrigerator colorful and easy to remove as you clean between your big cleaning times. On older wire racks they are great also because spills do not drip down to the next level. The mat catches it and you can easily wipe it clean. They also camouflage the not-so-good wire rack.

❦ Eggs stay freshest if stored in their original carton.

❦ Keep all lunch making ingredients together in a container; lettuce, sprouts, meats, cheese, etc. Just pull them out for easy lunch making the night before.

❦ Use turntables in your refrigerator. This helps to reach jars that get scooted to the back.

❦ Post a "to buy" grocery list on the refrigerator for all family members to add their needs and preferences. Your final shopping list will be easy to make. For maximum efficiency, organize a final list according to store layout.

BATHROOMS

❦ The bathroom is the most difficult room to keep clean in the house. Personal hygiene items are stored there. Too often, partial bottles of lotions, creams, gels, tonics and sundry items collect, only to take up important space.

❦ Remove everything from the cabinet under your sink. Use a handheld vacuum to remove hair. Using a soap and water mixture, wash inside your cabinets and drawers.

❧ Only replace the items that you use every day. Throw away all cosmetics and creams that are more than one year old. They can carry bacteria and create skin problems.

❧ Designate drawers for each person. One for your husband and one for you. Assign one drawer for all of the children if your space is limited.

❧ Store similar items together. Hairbrushes, combs and hairdryer, for example, can be stored in a plastic bin under the sink or in the same drawer.

❧ If you are short on storage space, display the bath towels rolled in a large basket. Hang a small half basket on the wall near the tub or shower for the face cloths.

❧ Box all first aid items in a sealed container and store out-of-reach of children (perhaps in the linen closet). Label the container.

❧ Toothbrushes can be kept standing in a decorative container on the counter for easy access.

❧ Use drawer dividers.

❧ Suspend a tension rod from wall to wall in an enclosed shower a few inches from the wall. This will serve as a shelf for shampoo and body gel.

❧ Store basic bathroom cleaning supplies under the sink for easy access. Buy smaller amounts and have a set for each bathroom.

❧ Use hooks for children's used towels.

❧ Designate an area for each person's used towel to hang so they can reuse that towel.

❧ Keep laundry baskets in each bedroom closet and make the rule that bathrooms must be free of personal items at all times since they are shared spaces. Toothbrushes must be put away, and soiled clothing must be taken to bedrooms.

❧ Store a laundry basket on the floor of the linen closet for soiled towels and washcloths.

❧ Keep a squeegee in the shower stall for quick easy cleaning. Swiping down the water prevents mineral build up and mildew. Even if you are the only person who does this, one time per day is enough for easy maintenance.

❧ Use containers to group items that are stored under the sink. Small stack bins are available in office supply stores.

❧ Colorful plastic stack bins can be placed beside a small sink cabinet to be used in place of drawers. My daughter is the stack bin queen. Her basement utility/bathroom is designated for her teenagers. The space is very small and the red stack bins keep handy face cloths, toothpaste, hair supplies, etc. She also mounted a decorative wall shelf unit which holds supplies that are displayed intermittently with decorative items.

CHILDREN'S BEDROOMS

The décor and the organization of a child's bedroom need to grow with the child. The place where the little tea table sat may now need a desk. Sort and revise as needed in this new reorganization plan. In today's home, children's bedrooms need to be multifunctional. Consider the function of the room and organize accordingly.

❧ Start with the closet. Remove all outgrown and worn-out clothing. Use the throw away/put away/give away system.

❧ Add stack bins in children's closets. They can be used for socks, underwear, shoes, T-shirts, and pants. It is much easier for children to help themselves from bins than to open and close heavy dresser drawers.

❧ If possible, add shelving to the ceiling of the closet for seldom used items.

❧ Utilize hooks inside doors and on walls.

❧ Mount high shelves on the wall of the room for display of photographs, trophies, stuffed animals, and collections.

❧ A painted bookcase unit works for containers of small toy pieces such as Lego's, puzzles, animal farms' parts, etc. These containers can act as bookends to books.

❧ A small desk will be helpful for school-age children. Store their art supplies and train them to do their art projects at their desk. Store their supplies; crayons, paper, glue, glitter, scissors and the like in small wire bins or colored boxes. You can even cover shoeboxes in color coordinating paper. If space is limited, stack them beneath the desk. Be sure to label them.

🍃 A hanging shoe bag is a great sorter for small items. It works for shoes too. The floor of the closet should only have containers on it. There should be nothing uncontained on the closet floor.

🍃 Store toys in a plastic laundry basket. It is easy to move from room to room.

TEENS' ROOMS

🍃 Use bins in closets for boys and retain a dresser for girls. Create a sitting area for a friend other than on the bed. You can place the bed in the corner against the wall and bank it with large pillows on two sides for a sofa effect. To take their same-sex friend to their room gives them a sense of ownership of their space. Help them keep it tidy but do not do it for them. Remember, you are training them.

MASTER BEDROOM

🍃 Reorganize your husband's drawers first. (You'll earn points!) Then do yours.

🍃 Fit dividers in the drawers. If you must, you can use shoeboxes.

🍃 Discard all old socks that are stretched out and have holes in the toes.

🍃 Throw away all stained underwear.

🍃 Rid yourself of anything that you have not worn in one year. Other than evening clothes, chances are you will not wear them again.

🍃 Equip a walk-in closet with bins or wire cubes. This will get everything off of the floor.

🍃 I hang my clothing by color rather than by item. But you can decide your own system. Most women organize their closet by item; slacks, tops, skirts, suits, dresses, etc. But I like to arrange by color. I tend to mix and match more this way. For example: All black clothing hangs together. My black slacks may be to the left; black tops next, then skirts, then jackets and finally dresses. Each color section will hang in this order.

🍃 Hang all of your clothing the same direction.

- Try to collect the same type of hangers. I like the clear hard plastic with the swivel wire hook. They are available with clips and without. Stock lots with clips, they come in handy. I try to buy at least one package (2 hangers) each time I shop at a "mart" type of store. This keeps my supply replenished.

- On your dresser-top provide a pretty dish for your husband to dump his things. On the nightstand keep a few pens in a small glass and a notepad nearby the phone. I keep a pretty candy dish with a lid on my husband's nightstand for his change. It is amazing how quickly it accumulates.

- Other items to have handy include matches or lighter for candles; tissue; a drinking glass or a small tray to set a bottle of water on.

- Under the bed can be a good place for storage containers to hold seasonal sweaters, seasonal hats/gloves, and skiwear, or extra bedding; blankets, quilts, and pillows. There are containers designed especially for under the bed and are labeled as such.

DINING ROOM

The dining room generally does not require a lot of organizing. The obvious china hutch, if you have one, will store your necessary dinnerware. However, I will give you a few innovative ideas for your dining room storage if you do not have traditional dining room furniture.

- If you do not have a buffet, use a low chest with drawers in your dining room for storage and a server.

- A "sofa" table will fill in as a buffet.

- Open shelving can hold stemware, tea sets, and even china.

- Hang seldom used linens on hangers and store in a nearby closet.

- Fold frequently used linens flat and store in a drawer or on a kitchen shelf.

- Line a drawer with a soft towel and store your cups and saucers in the drawer. Stacked cups and saucers are not attractive in a china hutch and take up too much space.

LAUNDRY ROOM

Caring for your family's clothing is an essential part of homemaking. Clothing is expensive, and if it is not cared for properly, it can be very costly for the family budget. Using proper supplies, good organization, and family cooperation can make this sometimes dreaded task hassle free. The time and effort expended in training family members in laundry basics are well spent. Listed are a few suggestions that will make your task easier.

- Keep your laundry area orderly.

- Store laundry cleaning supplies where older children can reach them. Depending on your space, you can use a utility cart, plastic stacking crates, or a mounted wall shelf.

- Provide sorting containers. Use plastic laundry baskets from the dollar store. They are lightweight and stack in a confined space when they are not being used.

- Enlist young children's assistance, sorting by color. You can begin as young as preschool.

- Label bins according to clothing type; denim, silks, towels and work/play clothes. When family members bring their baskets from their closet, they should then sort their clothing into the labeled baskets. When the basket is full, the designated family member should wash, dry and fold that load. Older children should be assigned the loads that require more care. Younger children can wash and fold towels, face cloths and kitchen towels. Train them young to do laundry.

- It is helpful to hang charts or information on laundering where others can check procedures before acting. Mount the charts on the front of the washer with a cute magnet. The following items may be included:
  - Stain removal chart
  - How to read clothing labels
  - Guide for selecting water temperature
  - List of basic steps to good laundering

- Provide appropriate supplies
  - Laundry detergent (use amount that is suggested on the container)
  - All fabric colorfast bleach
  - Fabric softener
  - Stain remover
  - Toothbrush for small stain scrubbing
  - Cloth to wipe clean the washer and dryer

- Trash basket to dispose the lint from the dryer
- A hanging device: hooks or rack that is mounted on the wall, over the door or on the back of the door.
- A few hangers

LAUNDRY TIPS

❧ Sort clothing properly.

❧ Check all pockets.

❧ Zip zippers.

❧ Do not wash towels with clothing. The heavy abrasive nature of terry cloth will break down the fibers of lighter weight clothing and will wear them out faster. The lint from the towels can create pilling on other fabric as well.

❧ If red clothing has never been washed, wash it alone to ensure that it does not fade. Some red fabrics will fade a little every time they are washed. Be very careful.

❧ Even when using a spot remover, most stains need to be rubbed a little. Be cautious not to over rub. You could damage the fabric and remove the color.

❧ Do not overheat your clothing while drying. Only towels can be dried with high heat. All other clothing should be dried on medium to mild heat, depending on the fabric.

❧ Fold your clothing while it is warm if possible. This eliminates wrinkles. If you forget a load in the dryer, when you are ready to fold it, turn the dryer back on for five minutes to warm your clothing.

❧ Do not overload your washer.

❧ If your clothing is not getting as clean as it should, check these items:
- Is the agitator in your washer working?
- Are you overloading your washer?
- Change detergents.
- Presoak heavily soiled clothing and socks before washing.
- Check your water temperature chart and follow it. Most washers have one printed on the inside of the washing machine lid.
- Be careful with stains. The wrong water temperature can set a stain the first time it is washed so that it can never be removed.

CLEANING—A VALUE OF GRATITUDE

*"She looks well to the ways of her household,
and does not eat the bread of idleness."*

PROVERBS 31:27

In the home where I grew up, Saturday was cleaning day. The bed sheets were changed, floors vacuumed or mopped, and bathrooms cleaned. The multiple changes of clothing from the week, which had been mounded in piles, were laundered and, once again, hung in the closet. Throughout the week, Mother was more interested in talking or "clowning" with us and making our favorite food than keeping a clutter free house. But on Saturday, she would clean and put everything back into place.

Spring-cleaning was a major undertaking! This was the time that curtains, windows, and walls were washed. We moved the furniture and even cleaned under and behind the stove and refrigerator. Was Mother a finicky housekeeper? Absolutely no! Did she teach us how to clean? Absolutely yes!

All family members should be responsible to keep a clean living environment as an act of gratitude. Caring for what you have is an expression of a grateful heart. The old adage "cleanliness is next to godliness" was quoted to us as if it was scripture. Don Aslett[1], says, *"How you live in and care for your dwelling shapes your personality—and your destiny."* If you were less fortunate than to have a mom like mine, you can still learn a valuable

thought from my mother. "If it is only dirty, don't throw it away—dirt can be removed."
So let's begin!

Cleaning Supplies and Tools
Here is a list of supplies and tools that are typically needed.

- All-purpose cleaner
- Bathroom cleaner
- Window cleaner
- Clean Paintbrush
- Window squeegee
- Cleaning cloths
- Treated dust cloth
- Rubber gloves
- Toothbrush
- Lambs wool duster
- Broom
- Dustpan

- Whisk broom
- Dry mop
- Old knife
- Sponges
- Bucket
- Vacuum cleaner
- Furniture brush
- Paper towels
- Kneeling pad/towel
- Hand scrub brush
- Toilet brush

ROOM-BY-ROOM CLEANING RULES AND IDEAS
EXTERIOR ENTRANCES

- Use mats outside of all exterior doors to keep dirt from coming into your home. Shake the dirt from them often, and replace them when they begin to look tattered.

- Sweep your porch several times per week. Sweep cobwebs from under the covering and around the doorframes.

- Wash the glass on the front door and on the storm door.

- Clean the outdoor light fixtures.

INTERIOR ENTRANCES

- A rug should be placed inside of each exterior door. It is best if this rug is washable. Shake loose dirt from them often, and also, wash them when needed.

- Clean smudges and fingerprints from the door edge, from around the door handle, and from the doorframe with an all-purpose cleaner.

❧ Dust all ledges including windowsills, tabletops, picture frames, wall shelves, and baseboards.

❧ Periodically clean silk flower arrangements by washing the flowers. Some arrangements or silk plants can be lightly swished in slightly sudsy water and drained. They will look like new.

LIVING AREAS

❧ Clear the clutter first. Then begin to clean from the top down, dusting cobwebs and ledges.

❧ Clean small knickknacks by soaking them in hot sudsy water. Immerse them first so that, while you are cleaning the room, they are cleaning themselves. Rinse and drain.

❧ Clean glass surfaces with a glass cleaning product and paper towels.

❧ Wood surfaces do not need furniture polish every time you dust. Use it once a month to prevent build-up.

❧ Fluff cushions and reverse them if possible.

❧ Vacuum window treatments rather than laundering them. (If they are aged they will fall apart.) You can also air fluff them by shaking them outside or hanging them on a line. Do not put them in the dryer.

❧ Sheer panels can be washed. You can replace them on the rods while they are still damp where they will air dry.

❧ Cotton sofa cushion covers can be washed. Use cold water to prevent fading and do not put them in the dryer. Put them back on the cushion while damp and prop them up to air dry.

❧ Apply stain prevention to your furniture and carpets to prevent spots.

❧ Always keep a spot remover stored in a handy location so that you can immediately treat spills quickly when necessary.

KITCHEN AND BATHROOM

- Always clean the surfaces with a disinfectant cleaning product.

- Begin by filling the basin or sink with hot sudsy water.

- Clean highest surfaces first and work your way down.

- Wash decorative items sitting on shelves. Wipe the shelves.

- End with the floor, using the following tips.
    - Clean on your hands and knees so you can wipe in places that a mop cannot reach.
    - Start in the area furthest from the door.
    - Wash the baseboards as you go.
    - End up in a doorway so you don't have to track over your clean floor.

KITCHEN

- Always wash counters with soapy water or a cleaning solution.

- Scour sinks regularly, then dry them. Clean stubborn gunk at the base of sink fixtures by wrapping the base with tissue and soaking with vinegar for 20 minutes. Remove tissue and brush away the remains with an old toothbrush.

- Clean the top of the refrigerator weekly. Place a cut lemon inside to freshen.

- Wash lids to canisters.

- Clean oven spills while they are hot whenever possible. Use a wad of dry paper towels. Then follow with a spray solution.

BATHROOM

- Scour tubs, toilets, and basins weekly.

- Daily remove hair from sinks and tubs with a damp tissue.

- A damp tissue also removes hair quickly from around the base of the toilet and from the floor. Do this between cleanings.

❧ Wash the back of the bathroom door. Because of the moisture, the panel ledges on raised panel doors can get crusty with hair and dirt. This is often forgotten when cleaning a bathroom.

❧ Clean shower door tracks by filling them with vinegar. Let them soak for a few hours. Flush out the gunk with water.

❧ Plastic shower curtains can be washed with a few towels. If they are mildewed add ½ cup bleach and wash with white towels. Do not dry. Hang while damp.

BEDROOMS

❧ Change bedding at least once every two weeks and pillow cases every few days.

❧ Store an old sock in the nightstand drawer and use for a quick dust.

❧ Use a dry, soft paintbrush to clean lampshades and picture frames.

❧ Disinfect telephones with an alcohol dampened paper towel.

❧ Clean an alarm clock radio with an alcohol based wet wipe.

❧ Clean under the bed.

FLOORS

❧ Vacuuming, mopping or hand washing your floors should be the final thing you do when you clean a room.

❧ Add whole cloves to your vacuum bag for a fragrant scent.

RAISE YOUR STANDARD

A friend of mine grew up in a family where her mother was a successful business woman. They were not rich but she had plenty. Her mother managed their home in the same efficient way that she managed her business. Housekeepers, gardeners, and handymen were a way of life. Her clothing was hung, laundry done, bathrooms cleaned, table set and dinner started, before she was picked up from school. Unlike me, she never participated in the process of cleaning.

The shock of her life occurred a few months after her marriage when her toilet bowl looked brown. She did not know what was wrong with it. She thought the whirling water when the toilet flushed cleaned the bowl. So she bought the blue stuff; now, it just looked dark blue! At 22 years old, she did not know that a toilet needed to be scrubbed. Be sure to include your children in the process of cleaning, even if you use the assistance of a house keeper.

You may reason, "Why should I make the bed when it will just get messed up again." "Why hang my slacks when I will wear them." "Why clean, it will just get dirty again." Yes, a clean house can and will get dirty again. But as Don Aslett said in his book, Clutter's Last Stand, "*...you can't mess up the improvements to the quality of life your efforts have produced.*"

Raise your standard of living. You and your family are worth it!

---

1 author of Clutter's Last Stand

HOME LIFESTYLE

11

HOSPITALITY—A VALUE OF SERVING

12

ETIQUETTE—A VALUE OF KINDNESS

13

HOME DÉCOR—A VALUE OF CREATIVITY

14

COOKING—A VALUE OF CONSIDERATION
Devi's Recipe File

HOSPITALITY—A VALUE OF SERVING

"Offer hospitality to one another without grumbling."

I PETER 4:9

A HEART ATTITUDE

The true meaning of hospitality lies in the attitude of the heart. Your attitude should reflect a desire to warm the heart and refresh the spirit of your guests. This attitude is demonstrated by your active presence as you direct your full, heartfelt attention toward your guests. All the planning and preparation should say, "I'm glad you're here!"

"…we were especially delighted at the joy of Titus, because you have all set his mind at rest, soothing and refreshing his spirit."

2 CORINTHIANS 7:13b AB

HOSPITALITY BEGINS AT THE FRONT DOOR

❧ A freshly trimmed yard, lovely front door wreath, blooming plants, and hospitality candles in the windows are just a few things that say, "Welcome!" as guests approach your front door.

❧ Always leave your front porch light on for guests.

❧ The foyer should have great eye appeal since this is the first part of your home the guests see.

❧ Avoid leaving muddy play shoes, gloves, umbrellas, schoolbook bags, and other items at the front door.

GREETING GUESTS AT THE DOOR

❧ Always meet your guests at the door with a friendly smile and eye contact to let them know you are glad to see them.

❧ As guests come inside, welcome them with open arms. A handshake or a hug will help to say, "You are important to me."

❧ Soft background music adds to the friendly atmosphere.

❧ Your guests know that you were expecting them if they see the table already set.

SAYING A SWEET GOODBYE

❧ Walk your guests to the door and be sure they have everything they came with—hats, gloves, coats, etc.

❧ When appropriate, give your guest something to take home. For example, when entertaining an elderly person who lives alone, pack containers with some of the leftover food and desert so they can enjoy a meal the following day.

❧ Whenever appropriate say a prayer with your guests before they leave. An edifying prayer of encouragement will warm their hearts and speak of your love for them.

❧ Walk your guests to their car. Wait until they leave the driveway before returning indoors. Send them off with a friendly smile and a big good-bye wave. This has always been a tradition in my family.

❧ Check the walkway for snow or ice in cold weather. Quickly clear a path. Offer to assist an elderly guest to her car.

❧ If road conditions are treacherous or snow covered, ask your guests to call you when they get home so that you know they have arrived safely.

🖎 If you are entertaining a single mom with small children, toys, and diaper bags to tote, always help her pack the car and get the children safely fastened in.

HOSPITALITY ENJOYED— HAVE FUN AT YOUR OWN PARTY
PLAN YOUR WORK, THEN WORK YOUR PLAN

🖎 Plan ahead. Make a "To Do" list and date when each task should be completed. Leave yourself a margin of time. Extra time allows for unexpected drawbacks.

🖎 Delegate work to other family members. Make it fun as you involve the children and your spouse in the preparation. This is a great way for your children to learn the art of hospitality.

🖎 Plan activities for your party. Volleyball, ping pong, board games or playing cards are a few activities at an informal gathering that can entertain just about anyone.

🖎 Itemize areas in which you will need assistance such as serving drinks, replacing ice, receiving coats. Select an outgoing, talkative person to help your guests get acquainted and mingle. Solicit your helpers in advance.

YOU CREATE THE TONE

🖎 The host and hostess always set the tone of the party. If they are happy and relaxed, their guests will respond in like manner.

🖎 Don't be worried or distracted. Remember the story of Martha and Mary. Martha was worried and distracted by last minute preparations. Jesus told Martha that Mary, who sat relaxed at his feet and visited with him, had chosen the better way. Luke 10:38-42

🖎 Complete tasks in advance so that you can be free to focus your attention upon your guests.

🖎 Keep a positive attitude. Avoid negative thoughts about your home, your own inadequacies, food preparation, weaknesses in your guests, etc.

AVOID STRESSFUL SITUATIONS

🖎 Maintain a peaceful atmosphere among family members as you prepare for guests. Stay calm and avoid harsh words or arguments.

⁊ Make sure you have more than enough food and beverages.

⁊ Know your guests' likes and dislikes. If you are entertaining a person who is diabetic or has food allergies, be sure to provide food that they can eat.

⁊ Be sure to have plenty of places to sit. You want people to be comfortable.

⁊ Stay relaxed about messes and spills. Although some spills must be cleaned immediately, others can wait until after your guests leave.

HOSPITALITY ATMOSPHERE
PREPARING FOR A TIME OF WARM FELLOWSHIP

Make your home inviting by adding special touches that will stimulate emotions and set a mood. Below are some suggestions that may transform your entertaining from an ordinary occasion to a memorable event.

ORDERLY HOME ATMOSPHERE

⁊ Your guests will feel most welcome in a home that is clutter-free and clean in appearance.

⁊ Wait to do the heavy cleaning and vacuuming after guests have left.

⁊ Try to maintain a clean and uncluttered kitchen, bathroom, family room, and living room as much as possible. In this way you are already prepared to entertain guests—even at short notice.

⁊ Sometimes guests come unannounced. If so, there is no need to apologize if your floor is dirty or your furniture dusty. Remember that the guests came to see you, not your house.

⁊ Do not continue to clean your house after guests arrive. Focus your attention on them.

CREATE A MOOD WITH FRESH FLOWERS AND GREENERY

⁊ Fresh flowers or greenery will be a spectacular addition to your table, counter, and/or living room. Experiment with different kinds of foliage.

- Choose what is in season. Use fresh pinecones, holly leaves, evergreens, or cranberries to add a cozy touch during the winter. Tulips, daffodils, lilies or other flowers can be used in the springtime. During summer months add flowers and greenery from your garden or purchase inexpensive bouquets for a beautiful centerpiece. During the fall season colorful leaves, unique squash, and mums furnish your home with a festive appearance.

- When on a tight budget, use summer wild flowers and greenery for a centerpiece. This same principle can be applied to the other seasons. For example, use pinecones and holly during winter.

CREATE A MOOD WITH MUSIC

- Music can be made louder when guests are first arriving to eliminate the awkward silences often experienced during introductions. After conversations get moving, lower the volume.

- Be sensitive when playing music. Do not have it so loud that the guests have to shout to be heard.

OUTDOOR PARTY

- Create a warm inviting atmosphere by adding special touches to let your guests know they are welcome.

- Keep food covered until you are ready to serve it. This will keep bees and flies out of the food.

- To keep things simple set up a buffet table in the kitchen or dining room. Have guests fill their plates and take them outside.

- Be sure you have comfortable seating for your guests.

- Be sensitive to the needs of your guests. If they seem to be bothered by mosquitoes or cold temperature, be prepared to move the party inside.

- Evening entertaining may call for outdoor lanterns, candles, music, tablecloths, and a centerpiece of fresh flowers.

HOSPITALITY IN RETURN
HOW TO BE A GOOD HOUSEGUEST

Mix and mingle. The most interesting person at a party is always the one most interested in others. As a guest you want to hear the words: "Come visit us again!" These guidelines will help you on your way to becoming the ideal houseguest.

ARRIVAL AND DEPARTURE

- Be considerate about being on time. Arriving too early may catch the host unprepared. Whereas, arriving too late may cause a great amount of inconvenience, even spoiling a meal prepared for you. If you are unavoidably detained, phone your host regarding your delay and when you expect to arrive.

- Know when it is time to leave. Be sensitive to the needs of your host. If the party ends at 10:00 p.m., don't stay longer unless specifically asked.

- When leaving, avoid making your good-bye lengthy. Some guests stand at the door and talk for another 20 minutes.

- Here are tips to help you recognize when it is time to call it a night.
  - Their children or yours are getting fussy. It is probably past bedtime.
  - Your host seems tired and is yawning a lot.
  - You are aware that your host needs to arise early in the morning.
  - Your host thanks you for coming and stands up.
  - If the host receives an important phone call or some unexpected event occurs, suggest leaving and visiting again at a more convenient time.

BRING A GIFT

- Be sensitive, trying to bring a gift suitable to the length of your visit.

- Try to discover in advance your host's taste or style.

- Some examples of appropriate gifts include a plant, food, specialty tea, flavored coffee, a book, a CD, boxed candy, or a gift basket.

- Avoid exotic gifts that may not compliment their décor.

HOUSEGUEST ETIQUETTE

- Do not bring animals with you. Make other arrangements for the care of your pet.

- Don't clutter. Whether you are visiting for just one day or staying overnight, pick up after yourself and your children. Ask where you can store your purse, diaper bag, coat, or other items so they will be out of the way.

- Train your children in advance concerning table etiquette, respecting the host's property, speaking quietly, not running in the house, and not fighting. Then remind them just prior to your arrival.

- If your young children make a mess, it is your responsibility to clean it up.

- Report anything broken or damaged to your host. Offer to replace the item and then do so.

- At an informal dinner, offer to help with preparation and clean up.

- When the host is trying to get the meal to the table, don't engage in intense conversation since meal preparation usually requires concentration by the hostess.

PRACTICE GOOD TABLE MANNERS

The Etiquette section of this book fully addresses table manners. Even if you have not become proficient in all etiquette rules, these are just a few, easy-to-remember actions that will put you at ease and will honor your hosts.

- Be kind. Kindness is the foundation for all etiquette

- Keep your hands in your lap when you do not have a utensil in them. Don't lay your left arm on the beautifully prepared table.

- Be joyful, conversational and complimentary.

If you forget everything else and just do these three things, you will have a wonderful time and so will your hosts.

OVERNIGHT GUESTS TIPS

* Travel light. Pack only what is necessary, but come prepared with your own shower kit, adequate clothing, pain medicine, antacids, and whatever else you will need to avoid borrowing items or creating inconvenience to your host.

* Keep the bathroom clean. After showering, clean out the tub or shower stall. Never leave hair in the drain for someone else to clean.

* Remove your personal belongings from the bathroom after each use. In some cases the towels you are using should also be removed to the room where you are sleeping to provide space for others. Be sure to put them on hangers to dry.

* Ask the host what time the day will begin. Never sleep in past the appointed time. You may delay breakfast or an early morning outing the host has planned.

* Make your bed each morning, leaving the room neat and tidy.

* Be sensitive to the host family's normal bedtime. Don't keep them up late at night if they are accustomed to retiring early.

* Maintain control of your children at all times. It is never the host's responsibility to watch or correct your children.

* Cancel the visit if someone in your party is ill. It is unkind to take sickness into someone else's home.

* Never throw a soiled baby diaper into a wastebasket. Bring a small plastic bag for used diapers. Ask the host where you can dispose of them.

* Offer to take your host and family out for a meal. This will give them a welcomed break from meal preparation.

* As a general rule never stay longer than three days. Have you ever heard the expression that after three days both your laundry and guests begin to stink!

> *"Let your foot seldom be*
> *in your neighbor's house,*
> *least he become tired of you*
> *and hate you."*
> PROVERBS 25:17 AB

FOLLOW-UP COURTESIES

❧ Always send a thank you card expressing your sincere appreciation.

> *"A word aptly spoken*
> *is like apples of gold in settings of silver."*
> PROVERBS 25:11

❧ Plan to extend an invitation to your own home. If you feel that your house is unsuited for accommodating guests, plan an outing in your back yard, at a park, or at a local favorite restaurant.

"My command is this: Love each

other as I have loved you."

John 15:12

ETIQUETTE—A VALUE OF KINDNESS

"Be wise in the way you act towards outsiders;
make the most of every opportunity.
Let your conversation be always full of grace, seasoned with salt,
so that you may know how to answer everyone."

COLOSSIANS 4:5-6

KINDNESS RULES

The foundation of all etiquette is kindness—people before policy. Kindness expresses itself with consideration for the people around you. Knowing proper etiquette makes you feel comfortable so that you can reach out to others and make them feel important. If you are concerned about making a mistake or appearing to be foolish, then your thoughts are consumed with yourself. However, when you know how to properly conduct yourself in the presence of others, then you are free to focus on them.

This etiquette section will focus only on proper conduct in the setting of the home, having a meal with family or friends. This is the place where we have the opportunity to make everyone feel special.

KINDNESS SUPERCEDES PROTOCOL

"...walk in a manner worthy of the calling with which you have been called, with all humility and gentleness, with patience, showing forbearance to one another in love."

EPHESIANS 4:1-2 NASB

Remember, people are more important than precedence. When we see that conformity to etiquette's code of conduct will embarrass someone, we need to adjust. We may, for example, host dinner guests who are not aware that it is our custom to thank the Lord for His provision before we begin to eat. When they begin to eat without praying, we can choose kindness over tradition. Rather than humiliating them by saying, "We always pray before we eat," we simply join them, finding another time to pray together.

PREPARING TO LAVISHLY LOVE

The host and hostess have a very solemn responsibility to practice the rules of etiquette. In doing so, they prepare a peaceful environment so love can abound to their guests. In the dominion of their own home they have the awesome privilege and biblical mandate to represent Jesus Christ to those who walk through their doors. Who knows, they may even entertain angels unknowingly. (See Hebrews 13:2)

"Practice hospitality to one another...with brotherly affection for... all others who come your way who are of Christ's body. And [in each instance] do it ungrudgingly (cordially and graciously, without complaining but as representing Him)."

I PETER 4:9 AB

THINK THROUGH THE DETAILS

Opening your home to guests carries with it a wonderful weight of responsibility. As host and hostess you will want to be diligent in your preparation, thinking through every detail of the visit in advance. If you are serving a sit-down dinner your readiness should be so thorough that both the host and the hostess are able to remain at the table during most of the meal. Always keep in mind that your visitors are there to see you. Your most important objective during their visit is not giving them a great meal, but lavishing them with love.

> *"Let each of you esteem and look upon*
> *and be concerned for not [merely] his own*
> *interests, but also each for the interests of others."*
>
> PHILIPPIANS 2:4 AB

SIMPLY PREPARE

Simply preparing things at the proper time, such as making the coffee or tea in advance and presetting dessert silverware, can free both the host and the hostess to be more attentive to their guests. Ask the Lord to teach you other ways that you can honor your guests. One of the things that I do is not found in any book of etiquette as far as I am aware. If we are seated at the table but I am only serving dessert—pie, cake, or something similar, I set the dessert and the dessert plates (stacked) next to my place on the table before my visitors arrive. Then, when it is time to serve the dessert, I don't have to leave the table. I can continue giving my attention to my company even as I am serving them from my place at the end of the table.

SETTING YOUR TABLE

The simplest part of your advance preparation is to provide your guests with the tools they will need to comfortably dine with you. Table utensils should be placed at predictable locations in such a way that they can be used one at a time.

- Forks should be placed on the left side of the dinner plate—tall fork near the plate and the smaller fork on the outside—while the knife and spoons are to the right—the knife is near the plate with the blade facing the plate and the spoon is on the outside.

- The salad plate is placed to the left of, or in the center of the dinner plate.

- The bread and butter plate is above the tips of the forks.

- The glass is above the tip of the knife.

- Dessert utensils can be served with the final course or placed horizontal at the top of the dinner plate. The dessert spoon handle faces the right and the fork handle faces the left.

- The napkin is placed to the left of the forks. Creative variations are allowed, provided that the napkin is never placed to the right of the dinner plate, in the goblet, or in the cup.

BASIC TABLE SETTING ILLUSTRATIONS

INDIVIDUAL PLACE SETTING

FAMILY STYLE DINNER

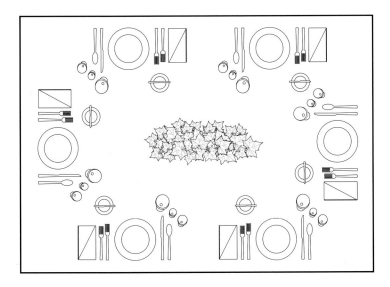

PROPER TABLE CONDUCT FOR THE HOST AND HOSTESS

SEATING YOUR GUESTS

- Seat your guests, alternating men and women. Since most couples are more comfortable sitting together, seat each lady to the right of her partner.

- Place cards make it easy for guests to find their seats, however, the hostess or host should be standing as they show guests to their assigned seat at the table.

- The host and hostess should sit at opposite ends of the table, never side by side.

THE HOSTESS SHOULD BE
THE LAST PERSON TO BE SEATED.

SERVING THE MEAL

- When the hostess is seated, the host should offer prayer. At the conclusion of the prayer, the hostess should give instructions to proceed, placing her napkin on her lap.

- If she finds that she needs to leave the table, she should tell her guests to begin. For example she may say, "Please begin while I bring the hot rolls."

- When serving family style, the host or hostess begins passing the food dishes first. They are passed to the *right—counterclockwise.*

- The host should assist with the refilling of the water glasses, giving the hostess time to take a few bites.

- The host and hostess should so coordinate their individual responsibilities during the meal that they can avoid leaving the table at the same time.

SERVING THE DESSERT

- Remove all soiled dishes and food items before serving dessert.

- When removing plates, remove only two at a time and do not stack the plates at the table. Carry them to the kitchen and return to remove two more plates until the table is cleared.

- Serve the hot beverage, coffee, or tea before serving the dessert. Guests can sip on the beverage while you are preparing the dessert.

- Remove soiled dished from the guests' right side and serve the dessert or dinner plate from their left.

AFTER DINNER

- If the dinner is formal the host or hostess should invite their company to join them in the living room or family room, leaving the dessert utensils on the table to be cleared at a later time.

- The host should encourage the visitors to take their drinks with them, offering to refill their glasses.

❧ If the dinner is informal and the company desires to linger at the table for conversation or to play a game, then the table needs to be cleared of dessert utensils.

PROPER TABLE CONDUCT FOR THE GUEST

There are rules for every stage of a guest's dinner experience. You can learn the proper way to conduct yourself from the time you are seated until the time that you leave the table.

BEFORE YOU ARRIVE

Ten minutes early and ten minutes late is considered to be on time for dinner guests. If you arrive any earlier, drive around the block and if later, call the hostess. Also bring a thoughtful gift to the hostess. This immediately expresses your gratitude for being invited.

WAIT ON THE HOSTESS

❧ Wait for the host or hostess to assign your place to be seated. Remain standing at your assigned chair until your hostess is seated. Then seat yourself, unless otherwise instructed.

❧ After being seated at the table, wait for the hostess and follow her leads.

❧ When the hostess puts her napkin on her lap, you follow. If she doesn't put her napkin on her lap, but begins serving, then quietly place your napkin and continue without making it an issue.

❧ Never rearrange the table setting—even if it is set incorrectly. Remember that kindness does not embarrass the hostess who did not properly set her table. Instead, we choose to bend the rule and feel comfortable doing so.

PASSING THE FOOD

❧ When dinner is being served continental style (the plates filled in the kitchen and brought to the table), someone will set your plate in front of you, serving from the left. After eating, it will be removed from the right.

❧ If the food is served family style, you pass it to your right. However, do not lift a food dish to begin serving until the host or hostess begins passing the food or instructs you.

❧ When serving family style, hold the dish for the person on your right to serve himself. He should then hold it for the next person and so on until it returns to you.

- To prevent accidents, avoid placing dishes on the edge of the table as much as possible.

- When butter is passed, cut a piece of it using the butter knife. If one is not set, use your clean dinner knife. Put the butter on the edge of your bread plate (if none is set, use the dinner plate). Never put the butter directly on your bread.

- Salt and pepper should be passed together at all times—even if someone says, "Please pass the salt." Always pick them up and pass them as a pair. The same is true with cream and sugar.

- When using sugar from a sugar bowl, do not use the sugar spoon to stir your beverage.

WHILE EATING

- If a water or beverage glass is garnished with lemon or other decorative fruit, place the garnish in the glass before drinking. The garnish is for enhancing the flavor of the beverage, not for poking you in the eye or swiping your nose.

- When eating bread, break off a bite at a time, butter it, and eat it. Never butter the entire slice at once. This rule also applies to eating rolls and using jam or other spreads.

- Always use your knife to cut. Do not attempt to cut food with the side of your fork.

- Never place a soiled piece of silverware back on the table. Rest it on your plate. If the plate has been removed, rest the soiled silverware on an unsoiled piece of silverware.

- Eat with your mouth closed, and do not talk with your mouth full.

- If you bite into a foreign object, simply remove it with your fingers and place it on your plate without saying a word. Do not spit it onto your fork or into your spoon.

- If you are served something that you do not eat, leave it on your plate and eat around it.

- Under no circumstance should you ask for an item that is not served to the table. If the hostess discovers that she has forgotten something, she will let you know.

- If you must leave the table for an important reason, ask to be excused. Return as quickly as possible. Your napkin is placed in your chair, not on the table.

❧ A centerpiece should not obstruct the view across the table. If it does, do not move it. Converse with the people who are beside you.

AFTER EATING

❧ When you have finished eating, place your soiled silverware in your plate. Even if some food remains on your plate, lay the utensils together and at an angle in your plate. The handles of the silverware should not hang over the edge of the plate.

❧ Thank your hostess for a wonderful time at her table. Compliment her for one item that she served. You might say, "Everything was delicious. I especially loved your pie."

❧ Do not overstay, and graciously excuse yourself when it is time to leave. Thank your host and hostess verbally and follow-up with a written thank you.

HOME DÉCOR—
A VALUE OF BEAUTY

"She makes for herself coverlets, cushions, and rugs of tapestry...
Give her of the fruit of her hands, and let her own works
praise her in the gates [of the city]!"

PROVERBS 31:22, 31 AB

SOMETHING-FROM-NOTHING DECORATING

Interior Design is a comprehensive degree that takes four years of college plus certification by a national interior design association to complete and to be recognized. While design has principles that can be learned, it is also an art form, making design both objective and subjective.

Anyone can have a beautifully decorated home if she can afford to hire a professional with a degree in Interior Design. But, hiring a professional does not always ensure that your home will be comfortable and wonderful. There are some things that no one else can do for you. Only you can mark your home with your signature and warm your home with your heart.

All creativity is inspired by creativity. Therefore, you will want to learn from other creative people. However, it is not a matter of copying what others have already done. Rather, it is the creative nature of God that He has formed within you which is released and expressed as others inspire you. It is then that you will begin creating as God intended. Try it!

Remember that if you love what you do, that is all that matters.

USE-WHAT-YOU-HAVE

Restoring the dignity of your home requires that you improve its appearance. The first step to improving the appearance of your home is to walk through it and evaluate the items you already own. You should maximize the use of what you have before thinking of buying new things. You can cause your home to come alive when you take a "new" view of your "old" stuff. In the end you may purchase very few new things, and yet, give your home a completely new look.

CHANGE YOUR LIFE-STYLE INSTEAD OF YOUR FURNITURE

If you buy new things and you are not taking care of what you already have, you will not take care of your new things either. If restoring the dignity and sanctity of the home were as easy as buying new furniture, we would all find a way to do that. But, there is a deeper principle. Consistency in caring for what you have can immensely improve your lifestyle.

Here are some examples of how you can improve your home by caring for what you already have.

- Free your home from confusion and chaos. Clear the clutter and keep it clear by finding a place for everything and putting things in their place after using them.

- Make your bed daily.

- Fold the laundry.

- Hang your clothing back in the closet each evening.

- Set a beautiful table, even when you are alone.

Master the mundane before you spend money to recreate your environment. You'll be amazed at the difference!

BEGIN AT THE BEGINNING

Start with one room. Thoroughly clear the clutter and clean it. Now, rearrange as many things in the room as possible. Change the placement of the furniture if you can. You may want to borrow items from other rooms until you make this room look as good as it can with what you have. If you feel, at this point, that you really need something that you do not have—a silk plant, a lamp, a pillow, or a picture—create a "wish" list for that room.

Make the list in order of priorities with an estimated cost of each item.

Maintain this new look and your new lifestyle in this room for at least one week before you tackle another room. Then, proceed to recreate another room until your entire home has been renewed.

Here are a few ideas of how to renew some of your rooms.

BEDROOM

- Try turning your bed at an angle. Place something tall in the corner behind the bed like a tree or palm, a pedestal with a plant on it, or a decorative screen of some kind. Now, let everything else fall into place.

- If your bedroom is very small, do not use a headboard. Place the bed in the corner using lots of large pillows propped against the two walls. Add small pillows in front of those. This gives a "sofa" effect to your bed in your small room. This works best with a twin, double or queen bed.

- If you want a headboard, simply use a sheet of plywood or pressed board cut to fit your bed. Do-it-yourself type hardware and lumber stores may cut it for you at no charge. Use a staple gun to cover it with sheet foam and fabric. Stand the padded headboard freely behind the bed. There is no need to try to attach it.

- Change how you have the top of your dresser arranged. If you have several small things, group them together on a tray (Polish up that tarnished silver tray that you got for a wedding gift!). Also, use trays to group cosmetics, colognes, and bottles of stuff. Add a small silk ivy plant and a candlestick borrowed from another part of the house. A similar effect can be achieved by grouping items on a doily instead of a tray.

LIVING ROOM

- Try angles. Pull your furniture from the walls.

- Place a narrow table behind your sofa.

- Set one chair with its back toward the TV.

- Clear your coffee table and put different things on it.

- Place your sofa and one or two chairs close to each other.

- Use an ottoman with a tray on it as a table in front of your sofa.

- Use seasonal live flowering plants for a long lasting "fresh flower" look.

- Group odd candleholders together. Gather them from other parts of the house.

- Group tabletop pictures in various sized frames together.

- Drape a table with a quilt.

- Roll magazines and tie with a ribbon or twine. Fill a basket with them.

- Paint a stepping stool a bright color and use it as a plant stand.

BATHROOM

- Nothing is nicer than a clean bathroom. Keep basic bathroom cleaning supplies nearby. Cleaning one time per week is not often enough for a frequently used bathroom. "Clean-it-as-you-see-it" is my motto.

- Dye old towels all one color. You must wash them all together when you do this.

- Hot glue a new trim on decorative towels for display.

- Roll towels to be used and stand them in a large basket if you have floor space for the basket.

- Hang a small basket on the wall near the shower or tub and put washcloths in it.

- Utilize unique containers to hold frequently used items like toothpaste and toothbrushes or cosmetic brushes.

- Place a small lamp on the counter with a grouping of decorative items mixed with useful ones.

- Use a set of plastic hooks for the children's used damp towels. Place the hooks at a level that can be reached, but be sure the draped towels do not reach the floor.

KITCHEN

- Use lots of color—at least three different ones—to create a color scheme.

- Spray paint old pots and pans using the colors of your scheme, and hang them on the wall.

- Keep a tablecloth on your kitchen table and use mats to protect it.

- Place several candles in your kitchen—one each on the counter, the island, and the table.

- Use baskets to store potatoes, onions and other root vegetables. These can be stored under the counter or displayed, depending on your space.

- Pitchers make great flower containers.

- Place a small lamp on your counter top or in a grouping on a tray.

- Frequently used cream and sugar containers can be displayed on a small, flat wicker tray lined with a doily.

- Paint your old cupboard handles. Each one can be different. You can also replace them with different kinds that are unique. Collect them one at a time.

- Drape old linen tea towels over a curtain rod for your valance window treatment.

- Always clear your counters of dirty dishes. If you must leave the kitchen before washing and drying them, stack them in the sink, place a sink suspended cutting board over them and top with a clean dishtowel and a centerpiece. This camouflages your mess until you can clean it. This technique must not become a habit. Use it only in emergencies.

- After using the kitchen sink, dry it with a towel.

"…Well done, good and faithful servant!
You have been faithful with a few things;
I will put you in charge over many things.
Come and share your master's happiness!"
MATTHEW 25:21

These are just a few ideas to get you started. I know that you are going to experience new joy as you look at your home differently and begin to use simple creativity to improve the environment where you live. You will be embracing the Use-What-You-Have principle.

ENHANCE WITH LIGHTING

Lighting is important to the mood that you want to create in your home. At times you will want brightly lit rooms and other times you will want to use indirect lighting. Don't forget candles. In all atmospheres, a lit candle adds warmth, serenity, fragrance, and friendliness. Consider a few creative ways to light your mansion.

❧ Place tiny lamps in unexpected places such as bathroom counters, bookcases, wall shelves, and kitchen counters. These are great spots and usually have outlets nearby. Add the lamp to a grouping and conceal the cord as much as possible. Keep these lamps on at all times. The small amount of electricity that they use is worth the enjoyment they bring.

❧ Light your entryways. If you enter your home from the back door or the garage, look for a way you can add a small lamp so you do not have to enter in the dark. Add a shelf or small table if needed. For your front entrance, keep a light on at all times. It says, "Come in!" to anyone who rings the bell at any time of the day.

❧ Most comfortable seating areas should have a lamp nearby. I like to use standing floor lamps and apothecary styled lamps beside comfy chairs so anyone sitting has adequate light for reading. Table lamps, although they are usually more decorative, are often not functional for reading.

❧ All bathrooms and hallways should have night lights.

❧ Add small shades to soften the sometimes glaring light of chandeliers.

❧ Paint old lamps and add new shades to update their look.

❧ Candles are essential. Use container candles for your everyday use. They do not have to be attended and are safe to leave burning while you are in another room. Never burn taper candles unless you are present in the room.

❧ Use candles for special effects. Line a staircase with glass contained votive candles for a special evening of entertainment. Fill a fireplace with wood logs and carefully place various sizes of candles on the logs. This effect is especially great when it is not the season to light the fireplace.

❧ Group several sizes, shapes, and colors of candles on a tray and use them for a center-piece on a coffee table or on the dining table.

❧ Light a candle in your kitchen while you are preparing a meal.

SMART TIP: HOW TO REMOVE CANDLE WAX FROM TABLECLOTHS AND CARPET

❧ Remove chunks of wax by peeling off with your hands. On an ironing board, place a large sheet from a brown paper bag. Lay the waxed area of the cloth on the bag. Place another sheet of brown paper on top of the soiled area.

❧ Press with a warm iron on top of the brown paper. Move the paper around as the wax is absorbed into the paper. Continue until there is no melted wax appearing on the brown paper.

❧ On Carpet: Remove all large chunks of wax with your hands. Place brown paper on top of the waxed spot and place a warm iron over the paper. Move paper back and forth until the paper absorbs the wax. Use several pieces of paper if necessary.

THE MOODS OF LIGHTING

Lighting should be adjusted depending on the function of the room. Consider the following lighting tips for the various moods and activities in your home.

PARTY

An environment of laughter and fun should have bright lights. Utilize all available lighting including overhead lights, lamps, and candles. Open window shades and blinds, even in the evening. Utilize outdoor lighting. If you are hosting a party in the evening, light your walkway with luminaries. You can make luminaries from a lunch sized brown or white paper bag. Weight the bag by pouring about one inch of sand or sugar in the bottom (sugar can be reused to avoid waste). Place a tea light candle on the sand or sugar and light. Always have your porch well lighted as guests arrive.

STUDY

A productive, studious environment requires a well lit room with direct lighting added to the table or desk being used. Blinds should be closed and distractions eliminated.

RELAX

The dim, indirect lighting of your small decorative lamps creates a calm, peaceful mood. Zone your lighting by turning off all lights in the room other than where you want to relax. Close the blinds, light fragrant candles, and play soft music.

READ

Read with proper reading light. It should shine over your shoulder and directly onto your reading material. Direct is more important than bright. The surrounding area can be dimly lit.

CONVERSATION

Soft surround lighting, using lamps and candles, is a great atmosphere for intimate or casual conversation.

MEALTIME

Light your table and dim all other lights in the room. Don't forget a candle. It makes any table setting special.

GAMES

A well lit room makes game playing more exciting. Turn on everything.

COZY

Indirect lighting with a few lamps (on low) makes a room feel cozy. The use of flames, whether from the fireplace or candles, gives warmth to the atmosphere.

MOVIES OR TELEVISION

Turn on your porch light and your entry light. Turn off all other lights except for your tiny decorative lamps in your bathrooms, kitchen, or hallways. Turn on one lamp in the room opposite your screen. Light a fragrant candle and be entertained. Turn on the hood light over your stove so you can quickly pop microwave popcorn without spoiling your theater environment.

PRAYER

Soft to dim indirect lighting soothes the spirit and helps one to focus on prayer. Light a candle and relax as you meditate on the Word and begin praying with a grateful heart. Brighter lights are great when rejoicing and praising. Appropriate music in the background directs one's spirit.

TIPS TO KEEP YOUR CANDLES BURNING BRIGHTLY

- Burn pillar candles no longer than one hour at a time for each inch of the candle's diameter. This will prevent tunneling.

- Trim wicks to a quarter inch before lighting. Trimming minimizes the size of the flame, which reduces soot and allows candles to burn more evenly.

- When buying candles, look for wicks that are well centered.

"Let each of you esteem and look

upon and be concerned for not

[merely] his own interests, but also

each for the interests of others."

Philippians 2:4 AB

COOKING—A VALUE OF CONSIDERATION

Devi's Recipe File

COOKING MADE EASY

When I began The Mentoring Mansion in 2002, I personally cooked and served the meals for my guests. I selected recipes that were easy to prepare, tasty to the palette, and elegant in presentation. I want to share a few of the tips that have worked for me over the years. By purchasing a few suggested seasonings and ingredients, you will be well on your way to a newfound cooking adventure. Be assured that cooking at home for your family does not need to be exhausting or time-consuming. While these are just a few hints for your consideration, I hope you will be inspired to try something new.

COOKING WITHOUT A RECIPE

Cooking without a recipe actually speeds the process of preparing a family meal. When you think about it, cooking is an art and baking, a science. Baking requires precise measurements for perfect results. With cooking, however, when you understand the basics of food and flavor combinations—like an artist understanding the principles of color—you can experiment a little here and a lot there to create your own tasty meals. This method of cooking allows you to prepare nutritious meals quickly and economically. You will soon find out that cooking without a recipe is learning by trial and error. This means you will need to make allowances for "error." Maybe your meatloaf with peanuts wasn't a family hit; I encourage you to try again. Your family will be blessed… the next time!

The following are tips for creating your own favorite flavors as you cook without a recipe.

FOOD AND SEASONING COMBINATIONS

SEASONINGS FOR BEEF

Salt and pepper

Red pepper flakes for hot and spicy

Seasoning salt or already mixed rubs

Garlic salt or powder

SEASONINGS FOR CHICKEN

Salt and pepper

Lemon or lime pepper

Ginger

Paprika

Cumin

Rosemary

Thyme

SEASONINGS FOR LAMB

Salt and pepper

Red wine vinegar

Oregano

Fresh Mint

SEASONINGS FOR PORK

Salt and pepper

Garlic salt

Barbeque spices

Onion powder

Cajun spices

Use your choice of spices listed above; pan sear the meat in a hot skillet with a small amount of olive oil, or broil the seasoned meat. You'll have a wonderful main dish in just a few minutes. When cooked in this way, meats create their own juices which can then be used to create a sauce or gravy.

GREAT STOVETOP MENU IDEAS

For quick preparation, slice the meat thinly (beef, chicken, or pork) and pan sear—like stir-fry. This method of cooking takes less time than baking.

Wash and cut red potatoes in small pieces. Leave skins on or peel the potatoes. Boil potatoes in water until tender. Mash the potatoes. Add onion in any form (caramelized, diced, sliced green onion). Add butter, salt and pepper to taste.

Steam a fresh or frozen vegetable. No measuring. No special ingredients. There you have it—a delicious, nutritious, and low-fat meal in 30 minutes.

VEGETABLE VARIATIONS AND GARNISHES

FROZEN GREEN VEGETABLES. Fold in a tablespoon of mayonnaise. Or serve mayonnaise on the side with freshly steamed broccoli spears or peas. Mixing one part mayonnaise to one part sour cream is also a good simple condiment for cooked green vegetables.

FRESH STEAMED GREEN BEANS. Drizzle with butter or olive oil and toss with sliced almonds.

CARROTS. Add any one or combinations of the following: butter, honey, fresh orange slices, brown sugar, and maple syrup.

VEGETABLE SOUP. Top with a dollop of sour cream and shredded cheddar cheese.

GRILLING VEGETABLES. Place fresh cut up vegetables in a hot skillet moistened with olive oil. Allow them to roast and lightly brown in the heavy skillet. Season the vegetables with lemon pepper or fresh lemon juice, salt, and cracked pepper.

ROASTED VEGETABLES. Cut a variety of vegetable into bite-sized pieces and toss with olive oil. Add salt and pepper. Bake in oven at 375 degrees until tender, 30-45 minutes.

MAKING SAUCES

Cooking without a recipe is easy when you learn the basics of sauce making. I recommend that you read about making basic white sauce and gravy from a basic, all-purpose cookbook. The *New Betty Crocker Cookbook* is my favorite. In the meantime, here are a few quick tips for sauce making.

FRUIT SAUCES

Orange Sauce: Begin with orange juice. Add sugar. Bring to boil and add a corn starch paste. Follow directions on the cornstarch box for the portions to make your paste. Stir until thickened.

Lemon Sauce: Begin with bottled lemon juice and dilute with water. Add sugar. Bring to boil. Thicken with cornstarch paste.

Raspberry Sauce: Mash fresh berries. Add water. Add sugar. Boil. Thicken with corn starch paste.

Now use your imagination with other fruit sauces. These can be served with meat or with a dessert.

MEAT SAUCES

Beef Gravy: Begin with pan juices from a beef roast. Place the juices in a pot on the stove. Skim off the fat. Add red wine if desired and/or water. Add a few beef bouillon cubes to enrich flavor. Boil. Salt and Pepper to taste. Thicken with cornstarch paste.

Turkey Gravy: Make the same as above except do not add red wine and use chicken bouillon cubes.

READ COOKBOOKS

Cookbooks are a fine source of culinary information and inspiration for combining different foods and seasonings. Study recipes, and then create your own version. Frequently, the first time I prepare a recipe, I follow it exactly. The next time, I create my own version—without the recipe.

From Devi's Recipe File

BREAKFAST

APPETIZERS

SOUPS

SALADS

SALAD DRESSINGS

VEGETABLES

ENTRÉES

DESSERTS

Breakfast

BREAKFAST SOUFFLÉ

BRUNCH QUICHE

FEATHER LIGHT PANCAKES

BRYSON'S CRANBERRY BREAD

MORNING GLORY MUFFINS

GERMAN PANCAKES
WITH LEMON SAUCE

MIMI'S BANANA–
CHOCOLATE CHIP BREAD

DANISH PUFF

BREAKFAST SOUFFLÉ

This is not a true soufflé but it sounds good. It is a popular brunch or group breakfast recipe and very easy to prepare. It has been in my file for many years. It is best to assemble it just before baking. I like to cook my sausage ahead of time and even have packets of cooked sausage in the freezer ready to go. If you do pre-freeze the sausage be sure to thaw it in the micro wave before using. Hot spicy sausage really gives this added zip.

6	slices cubed bread
8	eggs – hand whipped
1	cup sharp cheddar grated cheese
1lb	sausage cooked, crumbled, drained
2	cups milk (mixed with eggs)
1	teaspoon salt
1	teaspoon dry mustard

PUT bread cubes in buttered baking dish. 8x10 or 9x11
ADD the cooked, crumbled sausage over the top.
POUR egg mixture blended with seasonings over the cooked sausage and bread.
TOP with cheese.
BAKE for 40-45 minutes at 350 degrees.

Serves 8-10

BRUNCH QUICHE

This delicious crust-less quiche was served to us by our daughter-in-law, Kimberly Titus on one of our early visits to their home. Our son, Dr. Aaron married Dr. Kimberly in 1993. I seldom visit their home without asking for one of Kim's recipes. She is an awesome wife and a great cook!

1	6 oz. package frozen crabmeat or shrimp or frozen spinach thawed
1	cup shredded cheddar cheese
1	3 oz. pkg. cream cheese cut in cubes
¼	cup thinly sliced green onions
2	cups milk
1	cup bisquick
4	eggs
¾	teaspoon salt – dash of nutmeg

PREHEAT oven to 400 degrees. Grease 9" pie plate.
MIX crab, shrimp or spinach, cheeses, onion in pie plate.
BEAT remaining ingredients until smooth, 15 seconds in blender on high.
POUR into plate on top of crab, shrimp or spinach.
BAKE 35 – 40 minutes.
LET stand 5 minutes.

Serves 6 – 8

❦ ❦ ❦

FEATHER LIGHT PANCAKES

This recipe was in my first blender cookbook. It is the best "from scratch" pancake recipe that I have ever used. Since our children were young, all pancakes, whether they were in the shape of Mickey Mouse of Donald Duck were made with this batter.

1	cup milk
1	egg
2	tablespoons vegetable or canola oil
1	cup flour
2	tablespoons baking powder
2	tablespoons sugar
½	teaspoon salt

PUT all ingredients in blender.
BLEND till smooth.
POUR on hot griddle.
YIELD: 12 pancakes

To create special shapes for your pancakes, use large cookie cutters for molds.

❦ ❦ ❦

BRYSON'S CRANBERRY BREAD

When my grandson, Bryson, was in kindergarten, he excitedly brought this recipe to our house to make it with me for Christmas. Together we made it. Now it is a tradition to serve this for our breakfast bread during the Christmas season. I affectionately named the recipe after him.

2	cups flour
1	cup sugar
1 ½	teaspoon baking powder
1	teaspoon salt
½	teaspoon soda
¾	cup orange juice
1	tablespoon orange peel
2	tablespoons shortening
1	egg
1 ½	cups fresh cranberries, coarsely chopped
½	cup nuts

MIX together flour, sugar, baking powder, salt and soda. Add orange juice, orange peel, shortening and egg, mix until blended.
BAKE at 350 degrees for 55 minutes in greased loaf pan.

Note: Can also be made as muffins, with a shortened baking time.

❧ ❧ ❧
MORNING GLORY MUFFINS

I was a guest speaker in Tyler, TX when my hostess served me these incredible muffins. Of course, I had to have the recipe. It is now a favorite of mine. We opened The Mentoring Mansion with these muffins on our brunch table in 2002.

2	cups flour
2	teaspoons soda
¼	teaspoons salt
2	teaspoons cinnamon
1	cup sugar
2	cups grated carrots
½	cup raisins
½	cup chopped nuts
½	cup coconut
1	grated apple (with or without peel)
3	eggs
½	cup oil
2	teaspoons vanilla

TOSS dry ingredients, fruits and nuts together. In a separate bowl, stir wet ingredients; add to dry.
ADD ¼ cup or more of any fruit juice if too dry. *
DIVIDE between muffin cups.
BAKE at 350 degrees, approximately 20 minutes.

* These muffins will last very well without drying out and freeze well too.

GERMAN PANCAKES WITH LEMON SAUCE

I first was served this recipe while visiting the home of Bill and Nancy Carmichael in Sisters, OR. The Carmichaels purchased VIRTUE magazine from our ministry in 1980. Since then, this recipe has become a special occasion breakfast for our family. Whether it is at Christmas time or a birthday someone in the family always requests it. We also serve this recipe at The Mentoring Mansion.

3	eggs
½	cup flour
½	teaspoon salt
½	cup milk
2	tablespoons melted butter

MULTIPLY the recipe according to the serving size.

9 eggs = 6 servings
12 eggs = 9 servings

(When making a 12-egg portion, I use an electric mixer on low.)

USING fork, beat eggs till blended.
ADD flour and salt to eggs in 4 additions, beating after each.
ADD milk in 2 additions, beating well.
BEAT butter in lightly.
GENEROUSLY butter bottom and sides of a flat, shallow pan.
POUR in batter and bake at 450 degrees for approximately 15 minutes or until fully puffed. Reduce heat to 350 and bake for 10 minutes more.

SERVE with butter, powered sugar and fresh lemon sauce.

Accompany with bacon and fresh fruit.

DEVI'S NOTE:
I bake these in a non-stick, buttered jellyroll sheet. When I use 12 eggs, I divide the batter onto two jellyroll pans. A jellyroll sheet is a cookie sheet with side edges on it.

Lemon Sauce
I developed this sauce to serve with the German pancake because the heated sauce keeps the pancake warm. Adjust the sugar and the water to your taste.

¾	cup lemon juice (bottled)
¼	cup water
¾	cup sugar
2	tablespoons cornstarch
¼	cup water

COMBINE the first three ingredients in a sauce pan and bring to a boil.
MIX the last two ingredients together, in a separate bowl.

When mixture comes to a boil, slowly and continuously stirring, add the cornstarch mixture to thicken the sauce.

❧ ❧ ❧

MIMI'S BANANA – CHOCOLATE CHIP BREAD

This is absolutely the best banana bread recipe to be found. It came from a small tea book and was appropriately named Mimi's Banana Bread. Since this is what my grandchildren call me, the recipe seems like it should be original. My variation is definitely the addition of the chocolate chips. It has become a favorite at The Mentoring Mansion.

3-4 ripe bananas
1   cup sugar
1   egg
1½   cups flour
¼   cup melted butter
1   teaspoon baking soda
1   teaspoon salt
1   cup chocolate chips

PREHEAT oven to 325 degrees. Butter and flour a 9"x5"x3" loaf pan.

MASH bananas in a large bowl, add remaining ingredients and mix well.
POUR batter into pan and bake for one hour.

Note: Nuts may be added to the batter. You can also use this batter to make muffins, decreasing the baking time.

Devi's tip: You can freeze bananas that are ripening and use them in this recipe. The peal will turn black when frozen. Simply remove from the freezer, thaw under slightly warm water, cut off the end of the banana and squeeze the fruit out of the peal. You will always have bananas on hand for this quick-to-make recipe.

DANISH PUFF

This recipe is simple to make, slightly sweet, and elegant to serve. It definitely has a European appeal. It was given to me by a dear friend, Joyce Williams, when we lived in Wenatchee, WA during the early1970's.

PASTRY

1	cup flour
½	cup butter
2	tablespoons water

CUT butter into flour.

SPRINKLE with water and mix with fork. Pat thinly on ungreased baking sheet or pizza pan.

Puff

½	cup butter
1	cup water
1	teaspoon almond extract
1	cup flour
3	eggs

MIX butter and water in a small bowl.
PLACE butter mixture in small saucepan.
COOK mixture over medium heat until boiling.
REMOVE from heat; add flavoring.
BEAT in flour, stirring quickly to prevent lumps. When smooth, add one egg at a time, beating well after each until smooth.

SPREAD evenly over pastry.
BAKE about 60 minutes at 350 degrees in oven, or until topping is nicely browned. Puff has a tendency to shrink while cooling, leaving a custardy portion in the center.

Confectioner's Sugar Glaze

½	cup confectioner's sugar
2	tablespoons soft butter
1½	teaspoons vanilla
1-2	tablespoons water food coloring (optional)
½-1	cup finely chopped nuts

COMBINE confectioner's sugar, butter, vanilla, water and food coloring.
SPREAD sugar glaze on top. Sprinkle with nuts.
CUT to serve.

Appetizers

PITTSBURGH —
SUPER BOWL BLACK BEAN DIP
WITH GOLD TORTILLAS

ARTICHOKE HEART SPREAD

CRAB BALLS

STUFFED MUSHROOMS

🦎 🦎 🦎

PITTSBURGH — SUPER BOWL BLACK BEAN DIP WITH GOLD TORTILLAS

I found this appetizer on the internet by Chef: Greg Alauzen for a 2006 Super Bowl party held at the home of Scott and Brooke Sailer (my granddaughter). The black and gold hailed!

½	can chipotle peppers
3	cups cooked black beans (canned black beans can be substituted)
1	cup mayonnaise
¾	cup parmesan cheese
½	teaspoon chili powder
½	teaspoon cayenne pepper
1	teaspoon. salt (adjust to taste)
	Grated cheese (Monterey jack and cheddar)
	Chips for dipping

PUREE chipotle peppers and half the black beans in food processor.

COMBINE puree with remaining ingredients, except grated cheese.

PLACE in heatproof containers.

TOP with grated jack and cheddar cheese and heat in oven or microwave until bubbly hot.

🦎 🦎 🦎

ARTICHOKE HEART SPREAD

I was first served this simple but tasty artichoke spread by Pam Otto while living in Sarasota, FL. in 1982. It has become a quick-fix for me because all of the ingredients can be kept on hand. Now, years later, I have seen several variations to this very basic spread. Use your imagination.

2	cans artichoke hearts, chopped
1	cup mayonnaise
1	cup Parmesan cheese, grated
2-3	drops Tabasco sauce
	dash of garlic powder

MIX ingredients together and heat until it bubbles and turns slightly golden – approximately for 25 minutes at 350 degrees.

Serves 8

Serve with assorted crackers.

CRAB BALLS

I first tasted this recipe at a ladies holiday event that I sponsored in Harrisburg, PA in 1991. It is simple and quick to prepare yet a gourmet edge to it. The red color adds to a Christmas environment and if you garnish with green parsey, you have an edible ornament on your table.

1 lb. crab meat (imitation crab legs, flaked)
1   8 oz. Philadelphia cream cheese
    garlic powder (sprinkle)
1   bottle cocktail sauce

You can make you own cocktail sauce by blending ketchup and horseradish.

COMBINE cream cheese, garlic powder, ½ crab meat, 1 tablespoon cocktail sauce. Form mixture into a ball.
MIX remaining cocktail sauce and rest of crab meat. Mix together thoroughly.
SPREAD cocktail sauce and crab mixture over cheese ball.
CHILL well. Serve with crackers of your choice

Best if made the night before use.

STUFFED MUSHROOMS

While serving our first church, Bethesda Christian Center, in Wenatchee, WA from 1968-1980 we entertained often. House meetings and the ministry of hospitality was very important to Larry and me. I frequently served this appetizer.

2 lb. whole mushrooms
½   cup Parmesan cheese
¼   cup melted margarine
3   green onions, chopped
½   cup parsley, chopped
    garlic to taste
    Dash of salt
½   cup buttered bread crumbs

REMOVE mushroom stems.
CHOP mushroom stems, add all other ingredients.
STUFF mushroom caps with the mixture.
TOP with buttered breadcrumbs.
BAKE 5-7 minutes at 375 degrees or
BROIL If you broil, attend them closely.

Soups

DEVI'S VEGETABLE BEEF SOUP

CHICKEN WILD RICE SOUP

REFRESHING PAPAYA BISQUE

ONE-OF-EACH SOUP

❦ ❦ ❦
DEVI'S VEGETABLE BEEF SOUP

Since all of the ingredients except the meat are canned, this soup does not take long to assemble. It is ready to eat as soon as it is hot. The original idea of this soup was passed to me by my awesome sister-in-law, Shirley Titus, who has a wonderful gift of hospitality. Expectedly, this recipe has evolved to my own version, as most do.

1lb. cooked ground beef
1 can each of the following vegetables: carrots, green beans, kidney beans, corn, potatoes (cut in quarters) including juice from the cans
1 large can diced tomatoes
1 8oz can tomato sauce
1 small can tomato paste
1 large can beef broth
1 medium chopped onion
    salt to taste
    pepper to taste
1 T. oregano
2 t. basil
2 bay leaves (optional)
dash red pepper flakes

COMBINE above ingredients in a large soup pot heat on medium heat until cooked through.
I do not measure my seasonings but I am generous on all of them except the red pepper flakes and I just use a pinch of those. The measurement listed above are just to get you started.

SERVE with toppers:

A dollop of sour cream and diced green onion is wonderful. A spoon of Parmesan cheese is good too. Allow your family or friends to choose which one they like.

Serve with Devi's Herbed Pita Chips

Herbed Pita Chips
CUT pita bread into wedges
SPLIT the wedges
SPRAY or spread with melted butter
SPRINKLE with dried thyme and sesame seeds
BROIL until toasted

Note: These pita chips can be stored in a zip-lock bag and served at anytime.

✵ ✵ ✵

CHICKEN WILD RICE SOUP

This is a gourmet soup for sure. If you want to impress your guests or treat your family with the unexpected, this is a must. I think I clipped this one from a magazine and then did my own thing. I really enjoyed serving it to my SWAT sisters. (Only you will know who you are. Thank you for holding me accountable.)

2   14½ oz. can chicken broth
1   cup sliced carrots (I use the
    miniature carrots)
½   cup sliced celery
⅓   cup wild rice, uncooked
⅓   sliced leek or green onion
½   teaspoon dried thyme crushed
    (I use 1 teaspoon)
¼   teaspoon pepper

MIX above ingredients in soup pan.
BRING to boil; reduce heat.
COVER and simmer 50 minutes until rice is tender.
MEANWHILE, melt butter, whisk in flour. Stir in half-and-half or milk.

2   tablespoons butter
3   tablespoons flour
1½ cup half-and-half
1   cup cubed cooked chicken breast
2   tablespoons dry sherry

COOK and stir till bubbly, cook and stir 1 minute more. Slowly add half-and-half or milk mixture to rice mixture, stirring constantly. Stir in chicken and sherry; heat through. Do not boil.

Makes four main-dish servings or 8 appetizer servings

GARNISH with diced green onions, snipped fresh thyme (optional) and curled carrots (optional).

* Double the recipe for family servings and triple the recipe for "company". Gives plenty for refills. This is a great soup for entertaining. Serve with a selection of hearty breads and a dessert. Reheats well but be careful not to boil.

REFRESHING PAPAYA BISQUE

This is a great summer starter for your Indian Curry dinner or a new Thai recipe. Cool and refreshing. I clipped this during my travels.

4	ripe papayas, peeled and seeded (save the seeds for my Papaya Seed Salad Dressing recipe)
1	pineapple, rind removed and meat halved, cored, and cut into chunks
1	cup canned, unsweetened coconut milk
¼	cup dark rum – or ¼ cup white cream de cacao
¼	cup fresh lime juice
2	tablespoons powered sugar
½	teaspoon vanilla extract
2	teaspoons minced fresh lemon grass
½	teaspoon Sambal Olek (Indonesian and Malayan chili paste)
½	cup banana, peeled and sliced

PUREE in a blender, or food processor fitted with metal knife, papayas and pineapples in batches.

ADD and blend in coconut milk, rum crème de cacao, lime juice, sugar and vanilla.

POUR into large container and chill 30 minutes.

MEANWHILE, in a medium bowl, mix lemon grass and Sambal Olek. Add banana slices and toss to coat.

To serve: Top each serving of chilled bisque with a little of the banana mixture.

Serves 6

❀ ❀ ❀

ONE-OF-EACH SOUP

This is a party soup and definitely a conversation piece. The combination of the fruit mixed with the potato is the surprise. I serve this soup as a starter course in my antique-styled china creamed soup bowls. A creamed soup bowl is small and has handles on each side. Shallow soup bowls are for broth-based soups. It is a bit rich for an entrée` soup. I definitely acquired this from a gourmet magazine several years ago.

COMBINE

1   large boiling potato (½ lb), peeled and coarsely chopped

1   medium onion, coarsely chopped

1   celery heart (inner pale stalks with leaves), coarsely chopped (½ cup)

1   large apple (preferably Granny Smith), peeled and coarsely chopped

1   firm-ripe banana, coarsely chopped

1   pint chicken broth

ADD

1   cup heavy cream

1   tablespoon unsalted butter

1   rounded teaspoon curry powder

1   teaspoon salt

TOP

1   tablespoon chopped fresh chives

SIMMER vegetables and fruits in broth in a 3-quart heavy saucepan, cover, until very tender, about 12 minutes.

STIR in cream, butter, curry powder, and salt. Heat just until hot (do not boil).

PUREE soup in a blender until smooth (use caution when blending hot liquids).

THIN soup with water if desired and serve sprinkled with chives.

Note: Soup can be made two days ahead and chilled, covered. When soup is reheated, be cautious not to scorch it or to boil it.

Salads

CHUNKY CHICKEN SALAD

PEAR AND WALNUT
MIXED-GREENS SALAD

MOM'S CRANBERRY SALAD

SPINACH SALAD

❧ ❧ ❧

CHUNKY CHICKEN SALAD

This just happens to be my favorite flavor combinations for chicken salad. I like to serve it in a fresh pineapple boat. I guess I can say that it is original, but I'm sure I was inspired by someone to create this blend of flavors. It's fun to see my daughter and granddaughter serving the same recipe to their families.

6   boneless skinless chicken breasts
1   cup celery
1   small white onion
1   bunch green seedless grapes (whole)
1   cup whole cashew nuts
1   cup mayonnaise*
    salt
    pepper

BOIL chicken breasts, in salted water, until tender and cool completely.

CUT chicken into cubes once cooled.

ADD one cup chopped celery and one cup finely diced white onion, whole green grapes and whole cashews. Salt and pepper generously.

FOLD mayonnaise thoroughly into the cooled chicken salad mixture.

Note: The amount of mayonnaise may be adjusted according to personal preference.

SERVE on a lettuce leaf, a pineapple wedge or a melon wedge.

GARNISH with additional whole cashew nuts.

Serves 4 to 6 servings.

❧ ❧ ❧
PEAR AND WALNUT MIXED-GREENS SALAD

2	tablespoons butter
½	cup chopped walnuts
3	tablespoons brown sugar
	mixed salad greens such as Romaine, leaf lettuce, Boston lettuce
1	firm ripe pear (Bosc or Bartlett are good choices)
3	scallions, chopped
3-4	ounces crumbled blue cheese
	Balsamic Vinaigrette Dressing

MELT butter in heavy skillet over medium heat.
ADD walnuts and brown sugar.
SAUTE until nuts begin to soften.
REMOVE from pan to cool.
WASH and drain lettuce. Tear into bite-size pieces and place in large bowl.
CORE pear and slice into wedges at serving time.
TOSS lettuce, pear, scallions, walnuts and cheese with Balsamic Vinaigrette.
Serve immediately.

Serves 4 to 6 servings.

Balsamic Vinaigrette

2	tablespoons sugar
1	teaspoon dry mustard
½	teaspoon seasoned salt
¼	teaspoon freshly ground pepper
3	tablespoons balsamic vinegar
½	teaspoon onion juice (optional)
½	clove garlic, crushed (optional)
¾	cup salad oil

COMBINE dry mustard, seasoned salt and pepper in a small bowl.
STIR in vinegar, sugar, onion juice, and garlic.
JUST before serving, pour through a wire-mesh strainer into a small bowl to remove garlic if garlic is used.
BEAT in olive oil with a wire whisk.
POUR over salad and toss.

❦ ❦ ❦
MOM'S CRANBERRY SALAD

2   cups (1 package) fresh cranberries
2   cups sugar
2   packages raspberry Jell-O
2   cups water
1   cup nuts
1   cup celery
1   cup apples, chopped
⅔-1 cup crushed pineapple

GRIND fresh cranberries in a food processor and place them in a bowl.
ADD sugar and let stand.
DISSOLVE Jell-O and water over high heat.
LET cool, not thickened.
STIR Jell-O mixture to cranberry mixture.
ADD nuts, celery, apples and pineapples.
POUR cooled mixture into a pretty crystal bowl and serve from the bowl or store in refrigerator in a covered bowl and spoon into a serving bowl. This salad keeps well for several days.

❦ ❦ ❦
SPINACH SALAD

Fresh spinach, clean and crisp in plastic sack

3   green onions, chopped or thinly sliced red onion
1   dozen sliced mushrooms
5   slices bacon, fried crisp and chopped
2   boiled eggs, chopped
    croutons
    grated Romano cheese on top

See dressings for the dressing recommended for Spinach Salad.

Salad Dressings

PAPAYA SEED SALAD DRESSING

BLUE CHEESE SALAD DRESSING

SHALLOT VINAIGRETTE

✣ ✣ ✣
PAPAYA SEED SALAD DRESSING

My dear neighbor, Nancy Aprico in Wenatchee, WA during the 1970's gave me this basic recipe. Over the years I have created many variations and call it "my own."

1	papaya (seeds only) *
1	cup oil
1	cup white vinegar
1	cup sugar
1	teaspoon salt
1	teaspoon dry mustard
1	small onion

SCOOP seeds from 1 papaya into blender.
ADD all ingredients and blend.

Makes one quart. Store in refrigerator: Good on fruit or greens.

Variations of this dressing can be created by using different types of vinegar and omitting the papaya seeds.

My favorite combination salad with this dressing is:

Romaine lettuce
Slices of fresh papaya
Walnuts
Red onion
Crumbled goat cheese (feta cheese can be substituted)

Spring mix salad greens with strawberries, raspberries, or blueberries in place of the papaya are an excellent variation.

* Fresh papaya seeds can be frozen in zip-lock bags to use later.

❧ ❧ ❧

BLUE CHEESE SALAD DRESSING

Salad dressings for me are like scientific experiments. Some work and some do not. This one is a guess for the ingredients amounts. I just add until it tastes good. Feel free to adjust the ingredients portions to suite your taste.

½   cup crumbled blue cheese
1   cup sour cream
    double dash of wine vinegar
    Salt and pepper to taste
    Herbs—thyme, dill, rosemary

TOSS with greens or serve on the side. THIN with a little milk if you prefer a liquid texture to your dressing. I like a thick blue cheese dressing.

❧ ❧ ❧

SHALLOT VINAIGRETTE

This is a light vinaigrette that evolved from what I had on hand at the moment. Feel free to substitute shallots with a mild onion finely mined or grated.

½   cup chopped shallots
6   tablespoons seasoned rice vinegar
1½ teaspoons Dijon mustard
1½ teaspoons olive oil
    salt & pepper

WHISK shallots, rice vinegar and Dijon mustard in small bowl to blend. Gradually whisk in oil. Season dressing to taste with salt and pepper.

Makes ¾ cup.

Vegetables

BAKED ACORN SQUASH

FRUITED WILD RICE

GLAZED CARROTS

GRATIN DAUPHINOIS

BAKED ACORN SQUASH

I created this one but I'm sure I was inspired by something that I read. This is delicious and a fun way to serve squash. Even children will love to eat all of this vegetable.

2	acorn squash cut in half
1½	tablespoons packed brown sugar
1	tablespoon unsalted butter
	sprinkle of nutmeg
½-1	cup water

CUT acorn squash in half andj remove the seeds and membrane. Scrape until clean.
PLACE the cut side down in a shallow baking dish filled with about ¼ inch of water.
BAKE at 375 degrees for 45 minutes or until tender. Baking time depends on the size of the squash.
REMOVE from the oven and flip the squash over.
FILL the cavity of the squash with the brown sugar and butter.
SPRINKE with the nutmeg

Serves 4

Note: If the squash is large, bake it in the same way, cutting it in half. After baking the squash, cut in quarters, fill, and serve.

❧ ❧ ❧
FRUITED WILD RICE

The hired chef, Claire Comparato who is now a dear friend, served this rice with Pork Tenderloin at the opening gala dinner at the Mentoring Mansion in Youngstown, Ohio in December of 2002.

Since then, I have added some of the listed items to the old favorite Uncles Ben's original rice blend. Claire's creativity with food always inspires me to try something new— and different.

1   package wild rice to serve 6 persons (This is not a rice blend.)

COOK as directed on package.
ADD to cooked rice the following ingredients:

½   cup golden raisins
½   cup dried cranberries
½   cup chopped pecans
½   cup diced scallions
½   cup grated orange rind
½   cup orange juice
½   cup olive oil
     salt to taste

Serve ½ cup per person with a meat entrée.

❧ ❧ ❧
GLAZED CARROTS

I read this in a magazine many years ago. Please go to the extra effort to buy fresh carrots (the kind you peel). The flavor is to die for. Children love these because they are sweet. Great for holiday meals and so colorful.

1 ½   tablespoons packed brown sugar
1   tablespoon unsalted butter
½   cup low-sodium fat-free chicken broth
½   cup water
½   teaspoon salt
1 ¼   lb carrots, cut into 2 - by ¼ - inch sticks
1   teaspoon fresh lemon juice
2   teaspoons minced fresh parsley

BRING brown sugar, butter, broth, water, and salt to a boil in a 10-inch heavy skillet, stirring until sugar is dissolved.
ADD carrots and simmer, covered, until just tender, 4 to 5 minutes.
TRANSFER carrots with a slotted spoon to a bowl and boil liquid until reduced to a glaze (about 1 ½ tablespoons).
RETURN carrots to skillet and cook over low heat, stirring, until heated through and coated with glaze.
STIR in lemon juice and parsley.
SEASON with salt and pepper.

❦ ❦ ❦
GRATIN DAUPHINOIS

I attended a fun gourmet cooking class in Carlisle, PA and added this recipe to my collection. It's delicious and cuts in nice firm squares to serve. It is a gourmet touch to the loved scalloped potatoes.

2   lbs. waxy potatoes (red skinned for example)
1   clove of garlic
4   tablespoons butter
1   teaspoon salt
     pepper to taste
¼   teaspoon fresh grated nutmeg
1½   cup hot milk
1   beaten egg
4   oz. cream cheese cubed
4   oz. grated Gruyere cheese
¼   cup grated Gruyere cheese for topping

PEEL and thinly slice the potatoes. Arrange them in a baking dish that has been rubbed with a sliced clove of garlic and then well buttered.
COMBINE salt, pepper, nutmeg, hot milk, beaten egg and 4 oz. grated Gruyère cheese and cream cheese.

POUR over the potatoes and sprinkle with ¼ cup of grated Gruyère and dot with 2 tablespoons butter.
BAKE in a preheated 350 degrees oven for 45 minutes, or until the potatoes are tender.

Serves 6.

Note: The original recipe used 8 oz. of cream and 4 tablespoons butter for every 1 lb. of potatoes. (Too many calories!)

Entrees

CURRIED HAM

FILET DE BOEUF WELLINGTON

CLASSIC HONOMALINO
LAMB CHOPS WITH
PINEAPPLE PAPAYA MARMALADE

CURRIED HAM

I got this recipe from a cook book in the early 1970's. I have served it for more than 30 years. It is the opening meal for the Home Mentoring Intensives at The Mentoring Mansion.

1½	cups chopped onion
6	tablespoons butter or margarine
¼	cup all-purpose flour
2	tablespoons curry powder
2	10 ½-ounce cans condensed cream of mushroom soup
5	cups milk
12	cups cubed fully cooked ham
4	cups dairy sour cream
	toasted slivered almonds
	snipped parsley
	condiments

COOK onion in butter till tender but not brown in large Dutch oven.
BLEND in flour and curry powder.
ADD soup.
STIR in milk gradually.
COOK and stir till thickened and bubbly.

ADD ham and heat through.
ADD sour cream.
COOK and stir till heated through (do not boil).
SERVE with steamed white rice and top with condiments.

Serves 24.

Condiments
chutney (optional)
sliced green onion
flaked coconut
sliced almonds
raisins or dried cranberries

❧ ❧ ❧

FILET DE BOEUF WELLINGTON
with Blush Cream Sauce

This recipe was served to us during a brief time that Larry and I participated in a Gourmet Club. We met with wonderful people from diverse backgrounds in one another's homes and shared a meal, friendship, and recipes. Each time together was a new and refreshing experience.

1   6 to 8 pound beef tenderloin, trimmed of fat and silver (connective tissue), bring to room temperature

4   tablespoons oil

     toothpick, salt, pepper

1   16-ounce box of puff pastry (find in refrigerated case at grocery)

1   egg, beaten

1   tablespoon water

     fresh rosemary, garnish

     Duxelle

PREHEAT oven to 400.

SEAR Beef in hot oil on all sides in large skillet, approximately 5 minutes in all.

COOL Sprinkle with salt and pepper. Turn under tail of tenderloin and secure with toothpick.

COVER top of filet with thin layer of Duxelle.

ROLL out refrigerated puff pastry and completely wrap around filet, slightly overlapping where edges come together.

PLACE seam-side down on parchment – or aluminum-foil lined baking pan.

DECORATE with pastry cutouts such as stars, if desired.

MIX beaten egg and water to make egg wash.

BRUSH pastry lightly with egg wash, using pastry brush. Allow to dry and brush again with remaining egg wash. If first application of egg wash does not dry in 5 to 10 minutes, place in refrigerator for 5 minutes to dry.

PLACE pastry-covered tenderloin in oven.

BAKE according to desired doneness: 45 minutes for rare, 50 minutes for medium, 55 minutes for well. Remove from oven and allow to cool 10 minutes before slicing.

GARNISH with fresh rosemary. Serve slice of filet with Blush Cream Sauce.

Serves 12 to 14

Duxelle

2   shallots, finely minced

1   pound mushrooms, minced finely in food processor

1   tablespoon fresh thyme – or 1 teaspoon dried thyme

MELT butter in heavy skillet. Add mushrooms, shallots, and thyme. To make paste, cook slowly until thickened, about 5 minutes, stirring occasionally, cool.

continued on top of the next page

Blush Cream Sauce

1   cup red wine
1   tablespoon shallots, minced
1   tablespoon fresh thyme
5   white peppercorns
1   bay leaf
1   quart heavy cream
     salt

COOK wine, shallots, thyme, peppercorns, and bay leaf in skillet over medium heat until almost dry, stirring occasionally.
ADD cream and simmer until thickened. Stirring occasionally.
STRAIN through sieve into medium bowl. Stir in salt and white pepper to taste.

᠅ ᠅ ᠅

CLASSIC HONOMALINO LAMB CHOPS WITH PINEAPPLE PAPAYA MARMALADE

This recipe came from a Hawaiian chef and was printed on a restaurant promotional. I have had it in my files for many years and do not remember the chef's name. It is well worth making and grills very well too.

8   4 oz. lamb chops, frenched.

Lamb Chop Marinade

2   tablespoons soy sauce
2   tablespoons sugar
2   tablespoons hoison sauce (sweet-spicy soybean-garlic sauce)
2   tablespoons canola oil
1   tablespoon minced garlic
1   tablespoon minced fresh ginger
1   tablespoon cilantro
1   tablespoon minced fresh basil
½   teaspoon red chili pepper flakes
     salt and pepper to taste

COMBINE marinade ingredients and rub mixture into lamb. Marinate 4 – 6 hours in refrigerator, turning lamb occasionally.
BROIL lamb chops to desired doneness.
SERVE 2 lambs chops per portion with Pineapple Papaya Marmalade.

Serves 4 persons.

Pineapple Papaya Marmalade

16 oz.   peeled, seeded, diced papaya
16 oz.   peeled, cored, diced pineapple
4-5 oz.   granulated white sugar
1 oz.   salt

COMBINE pineapple, sugar and salt. Simmer in a heavy saucepan for 10 minutes, stirring occasionally. Add papaya and simmer for 5 minutes.

Desserts

CREAMED APPLE PIE

CHOCOLATE MELTING CAKES
WITH BANANAS

ITALIAN CREAM CAKE

RASPBERRY TORTE

CREAMED APPLE PIE

This recipe was first prepared for me by Star Asimakoupolus in Wenatchee, WA in the 1970's. It has become a traditional Christmas pie in our home. It looks like snow and is a very unique variation of an apple pie.

6-8 apples
1   cup sugar
2   tablespoons cornstarch
½   heavy cream
1   baked pie shell
½   cup coconut
½   cup walnuts

PEEL slice and simmer apples until tender
MIX sugar, cornstarch and cream in
   double boiler.
COOK until thickened.
ADD cooked apples. Remove from heat
   and cool.
POUR apples into one pre-baked pie shell.

Topping
8   oz. creamed cheese
1   egg
½   cup sugar
1   cup angel flake coconut

BLEND cheese, egg and sugar with mixer
and spread on apple filling.
TOP with angel flake coconut and
   chopped walnuts.
BAKE at 325 degrees for 15 minutes.

❧ ❧ ❧
CHOCOLATE MELTING CAKES WITH BANANAS

This recipe makes an impression especially for the chocolate lover. Accompany it with coconut sorbet or coconut ice cream served from a melon ball scoop and a few banana slices. It is definitely a conversation piece and is a wonderful choice when others are coming for dessert only.

8	ounces bittersweet (not unsweetened) or semisweet chocolate, chopped
6	tablespoons unsalted butter
½	cup all-purpose flour
½	cup plus 2 tablespoons sugar
1	teaspoon salt
4	large eggs
	additional sugar to dust the baking dishes
1	10-ounce package frozen sweetened raspberries in syrup, thawed, pureed, strained
2	bananas, cut into slices
1	pint coconut ice cream or sorbet (optional)

MELT chocolate and butter in heavy medium saucepan over low heat, stirring until melted and smooth. Cool.

COMBINE flour, ½ cup plus 2 tablespoons sugar and salt in large bowl. Using electric mixer, beat in eggs 1 at a time.

BEAT until mixture is pale yellow and slowly dissolving ribbon forms when beaters are lifted, about 5 minutes.

FOLD in melted chocolate. Refrigerate 30 minutes.

PREHEAT oven to 375 degrees.

BUTTER six 1-cup soufflé dishes. Sprinkle with sugar; tap out excess. Divide batter among dishes.

BAKE until cakes are set on top but tester inserted into center comes out with thick wet batter still attached, about 15 minutes.

COOL cakes on rack 15 minutes.

SPOON pureed raspberries onto 6 plates. Run sharp knife around cakes. Turn out 1 cake onto sauce on each plate.

GARNISH with banana slices and ice cream.

❦ ❦ ❦

ITALIAN CREAM CAKE

This recipes was given to me by Bonnie Coates. Bonnie and her family attended our church in Wenatchee, WA. Larry was the pastor at Bethesda Christian Center from 1968-1980. It was our first church to pastor. Bonnie baked this cake for us often. She knew it was one of the favorites of her pastor.

1	cup buttermilk
1	teaspoon soda
5	eggs, separated
2	cups sugar
1	stick margarine
½	cup shortening
2	cups flour
1	teaspoon vanilla
1	cup finely chopped pecans or walnuts
1	small can coconut

COMBINE soda and buttermilk and set aside.
BEAT egg whites until stiff and set aside.
CREAM sugar, margarine and shortening.
ADD egg yolks, one at a time, beating well after each addition.
ADD buttermilk alternately with flour to creamed mixture.
STIR in vanilla.
FOLD in egg whites, gently stir in nuts and coconut.
BAKE at 325 degrees in 3 7- or 8-inch pans. Cool. Frost with *"Cream Cheese Frosting"*

Cream Cheese Frosting

1	8 oz. package cream cheese, soften
1	stick margarine
1	lb. box powered sugar (3 cups)
1	teaspoon vanilla
½	cup nuts, finely chopped

BLEND first 4 ingredients.
FROST cake, then sprinkle more finely chopped nuts on top of cake.

❧ ❧ ❧

RASPBERRY TORTE

Joyce Williams served this to me in the early 1980's. It has become a favorite of mine. This cake is very elegant when it is served and is beautiful when it is displayed on a pedestal cake plate.

1   cup butter or margarine

1½   cups sugar

5   eggs, separated

2   tablespoons milk

2   teaspoons vanilla

¾   teaspoon salt

½   teaspoon baking powder

2   cups sifted flour

¾   cup raspberry preserves

1⅓   cup baker's coconut

2   cups sour cream (for low fat I use margarine
      and low fat sour cream)

CREAM butter.

ADD ½ sugar, cream well.

BLEND in yolks, milk, 1 teaspoon vanilla,
½ teaspoon salt and baking powder.

STIR in flour.

SPREAD into 3 9-inch round non-stick
pans greased or sprayed.

SPREAD ¼ cup raspberry preserves on each layer
to 1 ½ inch from the edge of pan.

BEAT egg whites and ¼ teaspoon of salt until
slight mounds form.

ADD gradually 1 cup sugar.

BEAT well after each addition. Continue beating
until stiff peaks form.

FOLD in coconut and 1 teaspoon vanilla.

SPREAD over preserves, sealing against the edge
of the pan.

BAKE at 350 degrees, 30-35 minutes until light
golden brown. Cool 15 minutes. Remove from
pans. Cool completely.

SPREAD sour cream between layers and on top.

GARNISH with preserves on top. In fresh fruit
season, I garnish with a pile of fresh berries in the
center and mint leaves.

CHILL several hours. It is not necessary to attempt
to "frost" the sides of the torte. This is not a traditional
cake and seeing the layers makes it special. Serve in
slight portions.

Serves 10-12.

"But everything should be done in a fitting and orderly way."

~ 1 Corinthians 14:40

"...being confident of this, work in you will carry it day of Christ Jesus."

that he who began a good

on to completion until the

Philippians 1:6

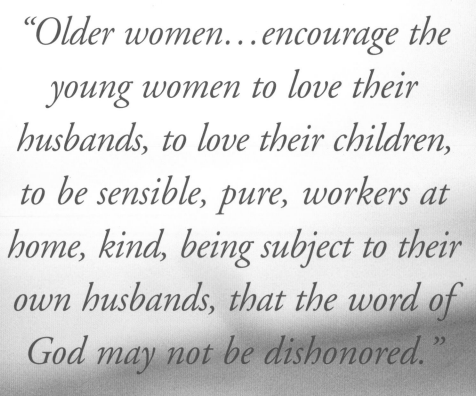

"Older women…encourage the young women to love their husbands, to love their children, to be sensible, pure, workers at home, kind, being subject to their own husbands, that the word of God may not be dishonored."

TITUS 2:3-5 NASB

A MENTOR'S GUIDE

15

PASS THE PRINCIPLES

*"So now I charge you…Be careful to follow
all the commands of the LORD your God,
that you may possess this good land and
pass it on as an inheritance
to your descendants forever."*

I CHRONICLES 28:8

A Home Mentoring Experience is truly a powerful wakeup call for you to breathe new life into your home. How? By restoring the worth and value God places on you, your home, and your relationships. Join women from around the world in winning back their homes for God and passing *The Home Mentoring Experience* to the next generation.

THE CALL TO MENTOR

Jesus said, *"…go and make disciples of all nations…teaching them to obey everything I have commanded you."* (Matthew 28: 19-20) Older women play an important role in this call. They have been given the awesome privilege of training younger women as noted below.

*Older women likewise are to be reverent in their behavior,
not malicious gossips, nor enslaved to much wine,
teaching what is good,
that they may encourage the young women
to love their husbands, to love their children,*

> *to be sensible, pure, workers at home, kind, being subject to*
> *their own husbands, that the word of God*
> *may not be dishonored."*
>
> TITUS 2:3-5 NASB

An older woman's example of obedience to God is what prepares her to train others to make home a place of love and peace. For women, these mentoring friendships are particularly important. It is not a suggestion or a question; it is God's design that each generation must give encouragement and guidance to the next.

If loving our husbands, nurturing our children, working at home, and being submissive came easily to all women, then we would not need to be trained in these areas. Instead, this scripture is a reminder to us that these behaviors must be taught.

WHY MENTOR YOUNGER WOMEN?

Younger women need encouragement and training. Why? So that *"the word of God may not be dishonored."* (Titus 2:5)   What does that mean? The *"word of God"* refers to the universal, timeless principles for wholesome living described in the Bible. When women do not place a high value on the areas described in this passage, they dishonor God.

For example, when a woman shows disrespect to her husband privately or in front of her children she dishonors God. This behavior sends a subtle message to the children that it is acceptable to disrespect their father. The rippling affect of this behavior is devastating.

A powerful example of how a woman dishonors God by disrespecting her husband is found in the book of Esther. Queen Vashti refused her husband's request to come to the banquet. King Xerxes was so disturbed by her rejection of his command that he asked his counselors for advice. They saw the widespread danger of her behavior and said, *"the queen's conduct will become known to all the women, and so they will despise their husbands...."* (Esther 1:17)   The counselors also said that *"there will be no end of disrespect and discord"* throughout the kingdom. (Esther 1:18)

It is vital that we do everything possible to avoid dishonoring God. If we are passionate about serving Him, then we must be open to instruction from a more mature woman. We are not to live independently. In this way the word of God remains pure and is not dishonored.

THEY DID NOT KNOW GOD!

One of the saddest verses in the Bible is in the book of Judges.

"After that whole generation had been gathered to their fathers,
another generation grew up, who knew neither the LORD
nor what he had done for Israel."

JUDGES 2:10

Why didn't the next generation know the LORD or what he had accomplished for his people? I believe it was because the first generation did not pass on their experiences and knowledge of God to the younger generation. We cannot make this same mistake. Make it your aim to pass it on to the next generation. Regardless of your age, you are "older" than someone else, and you can mentor them with what you already know. As you grow, others grow with you.

BENEFITS OF MENTORING OTHERS

"Two are better than one,
because they have a good return for their work:
If one falls down, his friend can help him up."

ECCLESIASTES 4:9, 10a

- By mentoring others you hold yourself accountable to practice what you have learned.
- You will have the satisfaction of knowing that you have helped someone else.
- Your friendships will deepen as you work, share, and pray together.
- You will have the joy of using what you have to serve others.
- You will play an important role in this fast growing movement to restore the dignity and sanctity of the home.
- You will be blessed by God for your obedience.
- Your home and family will be healthier because of your new life style.

THE STEP OF FAITH

Discover more than you dreamed possible as you commit to mentoring other women. Right now you may feel inadequate to mentor others. Don't be intimidated about training others. After you have spent some time revolutionizing your own home, you will be ready to share with others. Anyone who teaches another also teaches herself. As you mentor, you will receive back more than you give.

Our homes will always be improved!

"And day by day continuing

with one mind…breaking bread

from house to house…"

Acts 2:46 NASB

WHAT IS A MENTOR?

A mentor is one who invites you into her life. She encourages and trains you while modeling valuable life principles. The most powerful example of a mentor is the Lord's relationship to his disciples.

Jesus obeyed God, his Father. Then he said to his disciples, *"Follow me."* This simple pattern is what mentoring is all about. After Paul met Jesus on the road to Damascus his passion was to introduce others to Jesus Christ and to instruct them to obey. Paul used the same method. He obeyed, then said to those he influenced, *"Follow my example, as I follow the example of Christ"* (I Corinthians 11:1). The pattern is the same for us. We are to obey and then invite others to follow our example.

THE MENTORING RELATIONSHIP

This marvelous mentoring relationship is based on love and trust. The mentor shows love to those she trains and trusts in God to do the rest. This unique friendship is deepened by the genuineness and transparency of the mentor. The mentor's devotion and commitment will be visible by the gracious way she treats her guests.

The one being mentored must be willing to learn and receive kindly correction. No matter how good a mentor is, she cannot lead someone who does not want to follow. The younger woman willingly follows the example of the older woman in areas that pertain to her life.

THE MENTOR'S CHARGE

The most important responsibility of a mentor is to pray for those she will mentor. A mentor is a trusted older woman who comes along side of you. She trains and guides you primarily by her own example of obedience to God.

"Older women likewise are to be reverent in their behavior,
not malicious gossips, nor enslaved to much wine,
teaching what is good,
that they may encourage the young women to
love their husbands, to love their children,
to be sensible, pure, workers at home,
kind, being subject to their own husbands,
that the word of God may not be dishonored."
TITUS 2:3-5 NASB

❧ The mentor puts into practice the principles she will be sharing. She is careful not to neglect her responsibilities at home in order to mentor others.

❧ She is a peacemaker. She does not gossip, but instead, is kind and gentle to everyone.

❧ She uses self-control and avoids things in excess. *"Older women likewise are to be reverent in their behavior, not malicious gossips, nor enslaved to much wine...."* Titus 2:3

❧ The mentor does not let her emotions direct her life. Instead, she has learned to rely on God and to make right choices.

❧ She directs, inspires, encourages, and helps women in the difficult times of their lives.

❧ She can also be trusted with the secret fears, unsettling questions, and disappointments of those she seeks to help.

❧ She sets a positive example through her expressions of humility and love for those she mentors. She shares in the joys of the ones being mentored.

❧ The mentor's main concern is growth and maturity of those she influences. She cultivates a close friendship, yet she remains objective. In this way she can speak the truth in love when needed.

BIBLICAL TOPICS OF MENTORING

This list of topics comes from Titus 2:3-5. You will notice that our book addresses all of the areas mentioned below with the exception of addictions. For more information on that subject, please consult with your local church or book store.

- Speech
- Purity
- Kindness
- Addictions
- Self-control
- Orderly Conduct

- Loving your husband
- Loving your children
- Submission to your husband
- Caring for your home
- Workers and guardians at home

WHAT SETS A MENTOR APART?

Speakers, television hosts, authors, and world leaders do not qualify as mentors to their audience. These are teachers and authorities. They are not mentors because their role does not involve a personal relationship with those they influence.

Jesus spoke to crowds of thousands, but mentored twelve disciples who walked closely with him. He taught the secrets of the Kingdom to those who interacted with him daily. He took time to explain and help them to understand His ways.

This is what a mentor seeks to accomplish. She not only demonstrates how to make her home loving and orderly, but also, explains *why* it is important to do this.

AM I QUALIFIED?

You may feel that you are not qualified to mentor. Do not be discouraged. There are many women who do not know what you already know and are putting into practice. Do not think that you have to wait until you have your life in perfect order before you can help others. If we all waited for that day, then no one would mentor.

The Apostle Paul said, *"Not that I have already obtained all this, or have already been made perfect, but I press on…"* (Phil. 3: 12) So let's press on and mentor to the level of our own obedience.

WHEN CAN I START?

You can begin to mentor at any age. There is always someone else who is less mature or knowledgeable than you. Don't wait until you are older to begin mentoring. A nine-year old can mentor a six-year old to pick up toys and tidy up the bedroom. Teens can be great examples to younger children. A mother of adolescents can be of great assistance to a mother of toddlers since she has already experienced the early years of parenting. The examples are endless. Use what ever gifts, talents, and knowledge you already have to impact the lives of others.

> *"Stick with me, friends. Keep track of those you see running*
> *this same course, headed for this same goal.*
> *There are many out there taking other paths,*
> *choosing other goals, and trying to get you*
> *to go along with them."*
>
> PHILIPPIANS 3:17 MSG

17

HOW TO MENTOR— BUILDING STRONG RELATIONSHIPS

*"...the authority the Lord gave me (is)
for building you up, not for tearing you down."*

II CORINTHIANS 13:10b

Love is the key to building strong mentoring relationships. Nothing but love opens the door of the human heart and lets another in. Love is the most powerful force in the universe because God is love. Every healthy relationship has love as its foundation. When people feel accepted they begin to let down their guard. Then, they are in a better position to receive from you. Below is a descriptive list explaining what healthy mentoring relationships are all about.

MENTORING RELATIONSHIPS INVOLVE...

- A choice for the greatest good of another person.
- Serving others with warm hospitality.
- Forgiving and never holding a grudge.
- Letting go and not trying to control others.
- Interacting with transparency.
- Taking hold of teachable moments.
- Being humble, not boastful or proud.
- Caring, compassionate, and thoughtful actions.

🍂 Practicing patience knowing that only God can change a human heart.

🍂 Protecting the privacy of others by maintaining confidentiality.

The mentor's love for her protégés earns her the confidence needed to establish this special relationship. The emphasis is on helping the younger one to discover God's plum line for family and home. Mentoring relationships provide a fountain of blessing for those who give and those who receive. Anyone, regardless of age or experience, can benefit from these divine appointments.

THE APPROACH

Just be yourself. God wants to impact others through the personality He has given to you. Your approach will be determined by the younger woman's needs, personality, age, and circumstances. If you are mentoring a woman who is chronologically older than you, be sure to show her proper respect. If you are mentoring women of various ages and backgrounds, allow them to glean from each other. In other words, do not be concerned about having women of the same age, ethnic group, or similar backgrounds together. Variety will spice up the group.

Some mentors use a more direct style while others are more indirect. Be willing to adapt your approach to the needs of the group. Always using a direct approach of telling others how they should act and live can be offensive and distasteful. Instead, try using a softer, kinder, and less direct approach with certain personalities. A demonstration or hands-on method always works well.

CONFIDENTIALITY

When a woman confides in you, pray for wisdom as you listen to her. Let her know that anything she says will be held confidential—not even shared with your spouse or closest friend. The only time you should break a confidence is if someone is in danger. Both suicidal and abusive behaviors must be reported to the proper authorities. In these cases you break a confidence to help those who are being victimized.

TIMING IS EVERYTHING

There will be times when you may feel the need to *"encourage and rebuke with all authority."* (Titus 2:15b) Just be certain that you are sensitive to God's leading and timing. You may be right in what you want to say to someone. However, if your timing is wrong, the words will fall on deaf ears, possibly causing great offense or estrangement. By waiting for God's perfect timing you allow Him to guide the mentoring process and bring correction at just the right moment. Trust love to change a human heart.

NO PICTURE PERFECT MENTORS

Be careful not to compare yourself with others. There are no flawless mentors. Don't think you have to master all of your own shortcomings before you can mentor others. Relax! Trust God to help you accept yourself just as you are. Remember that He is at work in you and that your life is in process of being changed from glory to glory.

Learn to laugh at your own mistakes. Be vulnerable and transparent. Be willing to admit your own weaknesses.

Realize that women will observe how you: relate to others, honor your spouse, care for your children, keep your home orderly, and handle an array of other situations both good and bad. As they watch you, they are not necessarily judging or criticizing you. Instead, they are usually trying to find better ways of coping for themselves.

OWNERSHIP

Joyfully present and model wise instruction in the biblical principles set down here. Show love to everyone. Then, allow each woman the opportunity to choose what she will embrace for her own life. This style of teaching places the responsibility for change upon the recipient, not on the mentor. Remember that we have no power to transform another person. That is God's job.

Both the mentor and those who are being mentored are responsible for what they have heard. No longer can it be said, "I didn't know biblical principles for healthy living." Take courage and realize that you are not alone. You take the first step of faith and obedience. God will be there to empower you. The apostle Paul says to:

"Work out your salvation with fear and trembling,
for it is God who works in you
to will and to act according to his good purpose."
PHILIPPIANS 2:12, 13

WE BELIEVE IN YOU

Mentoring relationships grow strong as we believe in people. I, (Marilyn) have observed Devi's husband, Larry Titus, a gifted communicator, who has built several large congregations. He does not build great churches with strategies—he believes in people. His approach is much like Jesus. Larry believes that lives are touched and the world is changed by building one-on-one relationships.

Mentoring is all about loving others and realizing that everyone has potential. The Titus's infectious love for others has impacted more than 80 people who have been mentored by both Devi and Larry in their home over the past 40 plus years of ministry. Their passion has always been to uncover the undiscovered treasure in others. They love to show people how to improve their quality of life and to live free from negativity. "Larry has taught me the power of love—he loves people more than he gives them answers," says Devi.

"Whatever you have learned or received
from me, or seen in me—put it into practice.
And the God of peace will be with you."
PHILIPPIANS 4:9

18

HOW TO HOST A HOME MENTORING EXPERIENCE

"Contribute to the needs of God's people;
pursue the practice of hospitality."

ROMANS 12:13

The benefits of hosting a Home Mentoring Experience are huge. First of all, inviting ladies to your home for seven sessions will hold you accountable to the principles you have learned. Secondly, you will be sharing with others what you have learned. Not only will hosting a Home Mentoring Experience enrich the lives of other women, but it will also greatly boost your own personal growth. It is when you share what you have learned with others that it really becomes a part of you.

The Home Mentoring Experience is beyond description. It is a gathering of women who desire to gain wisdom from you, the hostess, as well as from each other. This home based experience will encourage women of all ages to change old habits, negative attitudes, and destructive patterns in themselves and their home environment.

In order for you to successfully mentor ladies, you must start by building trusting relationships with them. To initiate these special friendships you need to host the meeting in a home atmosphere. Your time together will promote closer relationships through the following activities:

- ❧ Sharing a biblical home principle
- ❧ Eating a meal together
- ❧ Learning a practical home technique
- ❧ Praying together

WHY MENTOR FROM A HOME SETTING?

Home is the ideal place for training because God's anointing rests on the home as His *Sanctuary of Love* for families. When home is the location for mentoring, all five of the senses are engaged. These include: seeing, tasting, touching, smelling, and hearing. Women are shown new ways of living a healthier life style. Ladies who are hungry to see radical changes made in themselves and their homes will be empowered by God and motivated to put into practice what they have experienced while in a home setting.

Mentoring from a church or seminar setting does not have the life transforming affect that mentoring from a home setting allows. Remember not to turn this experience into a Sunday morning or mid-week church meeting. If so, the impact on those attending will be greatly diminished. The synergy of this movement can only be felt as women meet from home to home.

THE HOME MENTORING GROUP SIZE

Keep the numbers small enough so that everyone can fit around your table comfortably. A group size of three to eight women seems to work well. Instead of having one very large mentoring group, consider a second group after the first one is completed.

MAKING THE CONTACT

Contact a small group of ladies whom you feel drawn to invite. These can be women from all walks of life. Do not limit the group to the same age group. The mix is a good experience for everyone.

Arrange to meet or talk with each woman individually. Begin by sharing with her your own experience of being mentored. Explain briefly how your own values and home conditions have improved as a result of this training.

WHAT TO SAY

Encourage each woman to join you in prioritizing her life—investing in herself, her family, and her home. Invite her to rebuild her home values by learning new skills and sharpening old ones. Share that the goal is to make your home *A Sanctuary of Love* and *A Haven of Peace.* Let her know that the time spent together will be fun, invigorating, and uplifting.

Also, explain to her the importance of being mentored. If she is a believer in Christ, share with her that this is God's design for an older, more mature woman to pass on what she has learned. Tell her about the Biblical mandate given in Titus 2:3-5. Older women are given the responsibility to train and encourage younger women so that the Word of God will not be dishonored. Hopefully, this will give her greater understanding of the significance of mentoring.

RESOURCES

Show each lady this book. Explain that she will reap maximum returns by having her own copy. This book is not designed to be read in one sitting, but rather to be digested slowly so that the principles can be assimilated and practiced.

Also, available are our teaching CDs (Devi Titus and Marilyn Weiher) sharing the principles given in this book. You may purchase all of these materials by visiting our website at www.mentoringmansion.com.

THE DATE AND TIME

Arrange a date and time for your Home Mentoring Experience that works well with those attending. Allow a 3-3 ½ hour block of time for the meetings. Meetings can be scheduled once a week or every two weeks. Meeting twice a month gives women time to make adjustments in their home lifestyle and maintains momentum for the next meeting. Meeting once a month is also an option. If your group decides to meet just once a month, be sure to make phone contacts with those being mentored during the month.

Ask women to be on time for the meetings. Let them know that they should call if they anticipate being late. This is a simple act of kindness on their part. Avoid delaying the meeting because someone is not on time. This causes inconvenience to both the hostess and those who made the sacrifice to be punctual. Always show respect to everyone by ending the meetings on time.

PRAY

Regardless of how well you know each lady be sure to pray for her prior to the meetings. Rely on the Holy Spirit to lead you in meaningful prayer. God knows our hearts and what each one really needs. As you pray for them, God will fill your heart with greater love and compassion for each wonderful person.

CREATE THE MENUS

Choose meals that are delicious, economical, and easy to prepare. Plan your time wisely so that you will not feel rushed or overwhelmed at the last minute. Many meals can be started a day or more in advance.

You may want to plan to give a practical demonstration of how to cook without a recipe at one of the sessions. If so, have the kitchen prepped with the ingredients necessary so that you make good use of the time available.

Each week you may want to ask someone to prepare and bring a home baked dessert. She can make her own favorite recipe and bring copies of it to share.

Suggestions for experiencing a variety of meal ideas include serving a buffet style meal, family style meal, brunch, special breakfast meal, holiday meal, seasonal lunch, or a lovely afternoon tea with small sandwiches and goodies.

Do not feel that you must serve a meal at every session. If a meal is not planned, please have a beverage and dessert or light snacks available.

SHOP FOR THE INGREDIENTS

Make a list of all the ingredients that you will need for your meal. Do this by creating a menu on the left side of a page and write down all ingredients needed for each dish on the right side of the page. Check your cupboards for the ingredients that you already have. Cross off these items from your list. Then, purchase nonperishable goods a week in advance. Other items like breads or fruits can be purchased the day before. Now, you are ready to do your shopping.

THE DAY OF THE HOME MENTORING EXPERIENCE
AN ATMOSPHERE OF PEACE

Maintaining an atmosphere of peace is critical to the success of this venture. Without peace there is no anointing from God. He is a God of order and peace. He provides us with his peace and expects us to walk in it. If you have been rushing around to get ready and are feeling stressful, this attitude will be felt by those you greet.

Using a schedule helps everyone to stay focused and to use time wisely. When planning the meetings, always allow yourself extra margins of time. If you discover that you cannot complete everything you have planned, focus on the most important areas. It is better to do less and maintain peace than to hurriedly try to complete everything scheduled.

One of the simplest ways to avoid stress is to prepare well in advance. Do not fret or worry. Keep a positive mindset and praise God even when things do not work out as planned. Expect the unexpected. Do not allow anything or anyone to steal your peace.

PREPARE YOUR HOME

The size of your home does not matter. Whether you live in a one-room efficiency apartment or a luxuriously large home, you can prepare your home for mentoring. Here are a few tips that may help.

Be sure that the kitchen, living room, dining area, and guest bathroom are clean and uncluttered. Choose the linens or mats, dishes, and glassware that you will use for your table. Preset your table before the ladies arrive for the session. Make it special with what you have. It is not necessary to purchase additional things. If you have cloth napkins, please use them instead of paper. Have the meal and beverage ready before guests arrive so that you are not spending time in the kitchen away from them.

If you have children that will need attended, please have them stay at the home of a friend or relative for the meeting time. This is good advice for the mentees also. Then, you can focus all your time and attention on your guests.

RECOMMENDED FORMAT

All of the sessions have a recommended format for easy planning of each Home Mentoring Experience meeting. This information will give you guidelines for each meeting. Also included are practical tips on everything from welcoming guests to closing a meeting on time.

"*Contribute to the needs of God's people;*

pursue the practice of hospitality."

Romans 12:13 AB

THE HOME MENTORING EXPERIENCE CURRICULUM

WE'VE MADE IT EASY FOR YOU

We have provided a curriculum guideline for those of you who are interested in hosting a *Home Mentoring Experience.* THE HOME EXPERIENCE is filled with exciting ways to turn homes into Sanctuaries of Love and a Havens of Peace. You will discover how to replace weak habits with life producing choices as you experience these important Biblical principles for today's woman.

Our purpose is threefold:
1. To mentor you
2. To provide you with resources to transform your home
3. To equip you to mentor other women

BRIDGING THE GAP

In every culture there is a need for mature women to guide and train the younger ones in essential home and vital relationship skills. Years ago most women learned everything from cooking to coping skills from a virtuous mother, grandmother, aunt, or close neighbor.

Today this type of transference has become almost nonexistent. Because of changes in family structure, in neighborhood relationships, and in workplace arrangements these valuable life skills are not being passed down from one generation to another. Hopefully, this book will be used to help bridge that gap.

HOW DOES THIS WORK?

You will be mentoring a group entitled a *Home Mentoring Experience*. This group will consist of a mentor, a small group of women, and a team to assist the mentor.

Every home meeting will be divided into two major sections. The first part entitled *A Sanctuary of Love* explains a profound and timeless biblical principle. The second part is entitled *A Haven of Peace*. It offers practical applications to equip women with valuable life skills.

We have provided recommended formats for use with seven sessions. These formats are presented later in this chapter. An experienced mentor has the option to adjust the format providing the principles are not compromised.

A HOME MENTORING EXPERIENCE MEETING

Expect each meeting to be exhilarating. Do not be anxious or nervous about this new encounter as a mentor. Tell yourself ahead of time that you will be open to what God has for you in this new experience. If you have small children, please arrange for child care in a separate location so that you and the others in your group will be undistracted.

You may serve a beverage, light refreshments, or a meal at the meetings. Be sure to let your mentees know ahead of time what to expect.

The length and frequency of meetings will be determined by each group mentor. We suggest that you meet every other week. This will keep the momentum going while allowing time for the ladies to put into practice what they are learning.

CREATE A SAFE ENVIRONMENT

True change in a person's life comes through an atmosphere of love and acceptance. During these Home Mentoring Experiences the ladies should not be asked to share anything highly personal. This is a HOME mentoring experience and not a personal counseling time. As the mentor it is your job to help create an environment in which the ladies feel safe, loved, and encouraged.

This safe environment is created by instructing everyone on the same level. For example, someone in the group may be an authority on table etiquette or home organizational skills. Yet, as the mentor you assume that they know nothing. That way no one will feel uncomfortable or put on the spot.

PRACTICE WHAT YOU HEAR

The easiest way to explain how our homes will be revolutionized is through the following familiar Bible passage. Jesus chose the home to give this powerful illustration which contrasts a foolish and wise home builder. They both had opportunity to hear the truth, but only the wise one chose to practice the truth.

> *"Therefore everyone who **hears** these words of mine*
> *and **puts them into practice***
> *is like a wise man who built his house on the rock.*
> *The rain came down, the streams rose, and*
> *the winds blew and beat against that house;*
> *yet it did not fall because it had its foundation on the rock."*
> MATTHEW 7:24-25 (emphasis added)

Please notice that a healthy home is built by those who not only hear the words of Jesus, but actually put them into *practice* in their everyday life encounters. Obeying God's commands is the foundation for a peaceful and loving home environment.

I would like to challenge you with this statement: Make it your commitment today that after hearing the wonderful principles in this book, you will practice what you hear. Don't let this happen to you.

*"But everyone who **hears** these words of mine*
*and **does not put them into practice** is like*
a foolish man who built his house on sand.
The rain came down, the streams rose, and
the winds blew and beat against that house,
and it fell with a great crash."

MATTHEW 7:26-27 (emphasis added)

Understand that it would be better for you not to know these truths and remain ignorant of God's plan, than for you to hear and not obey. Make it your aim as a wise home builder to continually put what you are learning into practice.

"A wise woman builds her house,
but with her own hands the foolish one tears hers down."

PROVERBS 14:1

BE PATIENT WITH YOURSELF AND OTHERS

This interactive mentoring experience is meant to encourage both the mentor and the mentees. Patiently allow space for trial and error. Anything worth doing takes time and effort. Guard against feeling discouraged or overwhelmed. God's power will see you all through this transforming experience.

"…being confident of this,
that He who began a good work in you
will carry it on to completion until the day of Christ Jesus."

PHILIPPIANS 1:6

A Home Mentoring Experience with Seven Sessions

Following are the recommended formats for you to use when you invite others to your home to host a *Home Mentoring Experience.* These formats are exactly what I have called them—a recommendation. Feel free to adjust and adapt them to your personal preference. They are merely meant to be guidelines.

SESSION 1 – RECOMMENDED FORMAT

ALLOW 3 HOURS AND 15 MINUTES FOR THIS SESSION.

15 minutes	Greeting and Introduction
60 minutes	Dining—Share a Meal Together (Optional)*
	Ch. 12 Etiquette—A Value of Kindness

A SANCTUARY OF LOVE

45 minutes	Ch. 1 The Dignity and Sanctity of the Home
30 minutes	Discussion

A HAVEN OF PEACE

30 minutes	Ch. 13 Home Décor—Enhance with Lighting
15 minutes	Closing

STEP ONE: 15 MINUTES—GREETING AND INTRODUCTION

Welcome each guest enthusiastically as you greet them at the front door. Lead them into the living room/family room for the introduction. In a few words, tell them what THE HOME EXPERIENCE has meant to you and why you have asked them to come. Share with them that they will have the opportunity to transform their homes.

Let them know that, although some may already be well trained in certain areas, you will teach everyone as if they are beginners. In this way, everyone can be instructed from the ground level, and no one will feel inadequate. Also, explain that they will be learning through all five of their senses—tasting, touching, smelling, seeing, and hearing.

Play a name game if the guests do not know each other. Here is one that is used at The Mentoring Mansion. Ask each woman to give her name and state an adjective beginning with the first letter of her name. The word chosen must describe something positive about her. For example: Decisive Debbie, Joyful Janet, Caring Carol. The next woman will start by repeating the adjectives and names of the previous women. Then she will give her own. Tell them that this is not a test. Let everyone help and watch how quickly you can remember the names.

STEP TWO: 60 MINUTES—THE MEAL TIME AT THE TABLE
Sharing a meal together brings people together and strengthens relationships. An informal buffet-style meal is a great way to begin. If the women do not know each other, use the first part of your meal to get acquainted. Ask each woman to share briefly something about herself such as: marital status, children's ages, and vocation.

* Make a meal for your guests if your finances permit. If this is not feasible, here are some other options you may want to consider:
  * Share the meal preparation and expense with another woman
  * Provide a beverage and a dessert
  * Offer healthy snacks or finger foods

TABLE TIME INSTRUCTION: CHAPTER 12 ETIQUETTE Share with the ladies some of the important details from Chapter 12 Etiquette—A Value of Kindness. This can be done while sharing a meal or dessert together. The ladies do not need to have their books with them during this time.

CURRICULUM: A SANCTUARY OF LOVE
STEP THREE: 45 MINUTES—CHAPTER 1 Move to the living room or family room. The mentor may talk about the principles found in Chapter 1, *Dignity and Sanctity of the Home*, or play the CD that accompanies this section.

STEP FOUR: 30 MINUTES—DISCUSSION TIME Allow for some brief discussion about *The Dignity and Sanctity of the Home*. Remember to stay focused and stay within the allotted time frame.

CURRICULUM: A HAVEN OF PEACE

STEP FIVE: 30 MINUTES—
CREATIVE HOME SKILL DEMONSTRATION

The Home Order section of the book offers practical suggestions to enhance the beauty of your home. You may choose to use the material found in Chapter 12 entitled: Enhance with Lighting. This describes how you can use lighting to create different moods.

Here are some other ideas you can choose from: home decorating, front door decorating, room arranging, organizing a closet, organizing a child's room, cooking tips, cleaning tips, holiday decorating, economical shopping, gardening, using herbs in cooking, and making window treatments.

Surely there is someone you know who would be willing to give a brief demonstration of one of these areas mentioned above. Do not feel that you must be skilled in all these areas. Give yourself a break and involve others who are creative and love to share their talents.

STEP SIX: 15 MINUTES—CLOSING

Announce the date of the next meeting. Ask them to read Chapter 4 entitled The Table Principle. Remind the ladies to bring their books and their Bibles to each meeting. Conclude the evening with a smile, a hug, and a word of thanks for coming.

Do not encourage guests to linger long after the meeting is over. End on time. Remember this important courtesy for your guests and their families as well as your own.

How do you get everyone's cooperation to leave on time? You can politely stand up to suggest that the meeting is at a close. You may want to end with a brief prayer, then get their coats, and graciously walk them to the door. However, please be sensitive to the needs of each lady. If you feel that there is someone who needs extra time and attention you can make arrangements to meet with her at another time.

SESSION 2 – RECOMMENDED FORMAT

> ***ALLOW 3 HOURS FOR THIS SESSION***
>
> 10 minutes   Greeting
>
> **A SANCTUARY OF LOVE**
>
> 60 minutes   Ch. 4 The Table Principle
>
> 15 minutes   Discussion
>
> 45 minutes   Informal style meal
>
> **A HAVEN OF PEACE**
>
> 15 minutes   Ch. 12 Etiquette
>
> 25 minutes   Ch. 9 Home Organization
>
> 10 minutes   Closing

STEP ONE: 10 MINUTES—GREETING

Welcome each guest enthusiastically as you greet each one at the front door.

CURRICULUM: A SANCTUARY OF LOVE

STEP TWO: 60 MINUTES—CHAPTER 4

Move to the living room or family room. Talk about the principles found in Chapter 4, the Table Principle, or play the accompanying CD.

STEP THREE: 15 MINUTES—DISCUSSION

Allow for some discussion time afterward. If the ladies have already read this section before attending the meeting, they may want to share a little from their study guide.

STEP FOUR: 45 MINUTES—MEAL TIME

This meal can be an informal brunch or luncheon served buffet style. We do not want you to turn The Table Principle into a rigid, legalistic practice requiring them to always eat meals at a table. Therefore, after teaching The Table Principle you may want to have the women take their plates into the living room or family room.

CURRICULUM: A HAVEN OF PEACE
STEP FIVE: 15 MINUTES—CHAPTER 12
After this meal discuss the etiquette of preparing for guests. This information can be found in Chapter 12, Etiquette: Preparing for Guests.

STEP SIX: 25 MINUTES—CHAPTER 9
Ask the ladies to turn to Chapter 9 Home Organization. Briefly review and touch on the ones you feel are most important for your group. Also, you can use this time to walk the ladies from room to room showing how you have organized specific areas of your home. Do not feel like you have to show every area. Simply choose what areas you want to demonstrate. For example, you may start in the kitchen demonstrating a drawer, a cupboard, or pantry area. Then move to the laundry room, a bedroom, or a closet in like manner.

STEP SEVEN: 15 MINUTES—CLOSING
Announce the date of the next meeting. Ask them to read Chapter 7 entitled Honoring Your Husband. Please remind them to bring their book and Bible to each meeting. Conclude the evening with a smile, a hug, and a word of thanks for coming. Remember to end on time.

SESSION 3 – RECOMMENDED FORMAT

ALLOW 3 HOURS FOR THIS SESSION

10 minutes	Greeting
60 minutes	Family style meal or a dessert
A SANCTUARY OF LOVE	
60 minutes	Ch. 7 Honoring Your Husband
30 minutes	Discussion
A HAVEN OF PEACE	
25 minutes	Ch. 10 Ten Smart Cleaning Tips
	Ch. 11 Hospitality
10 minutes	Closing

STEP ONE: 15 MINUTES—GREETING

Welcome each guest enthusiastically as you greet them at the front door. Lead them to your table.

STEP TWO: 60 MINUTES—MEAL TIME

Have the table preset before guests arrive. You can serve family style where the food is placed on the table. If you choose this style, tell them the kindness rule of passing food dishes to the right. Another idea is to have the plates filled from the kitchen and brought to the table after all guests have been seated.

CURRICULUM: A SANCTUARY OF LOVE

STEP THREE: 60 MINUTES—CHAPTER 7

Move to the meeting room. The mentor may talk about the principles found in Chapter 7, Honoring Your Husband, or play the CD that accompanies this section.

STEP FOUR: 30 MINUTES—DISCUSSION AND PRAYER

Allow for positive discussion time. The ladies may want to discuss topics from their study guide during this time. I always like to pray for the husband-wife relationships that are represented at the meeting.

CURRICULUM: HAVEN OF PEACE
STEP FIVE: 25 MINUTES—CHAPTER 10

Ask the ladies to turn to Chapter 10, Ten Smart Cleaning Tips. Briefly go over some of the ten tips. Share some specific cleaning tips that work for you. Some ladies may want to add some of their own cleaning tips. Be creative. This could be presented as a brief demonstration.

STEP SIX: CHAPTER 11

If possible change locations in your home for instruction on Chapter 11, Hospitality Tips— a value of serving.

STEP SEVEN: 10 MINUTES—CLOSING

Announce the date of the next meeting. Remind them to read Chapter 2 The Also Principle. Conclude the evening with a smile, a hug, and a word of thanks for coming. Remember to end on time.

SESSION 4 – RECOMMENDED FORMAT
FINAL SESSION

ALLOW 3 HOURS AND 15 MINUTES FOR THIS SESSION

10 minutes	Greeting

A HAVEN OF PEACE

60 minutes	Ch. 14 Cooking Without a Recipe Demonstration
45 minutes	Dining
15 minutes	Ten Smart Cooking Tips

A SANCTUARY OF LOVE

45 minutes	Ch. 2 The Also Principle
15 minutes	Discussion
5 minutes	Closing

STEP ONE: 10 MINUTES—GREETING

Welcome each guest enthusiastically as you greet them at the front door. Lead them into the kitchen.

CURRICULUM: A HAVEN OF PEACE
STEP TWO: 60 MINUTES—CHAPTER 14

Have the table preset before guests arrive. The plates can be filled from the kitchen and brought to the table. Each guest can carry her own plate from the kitchen to the table.

Give a demonstration of Cooking Without a Recipe. Show the women how to prepare a meal without a recipe. This meal needs to be one which can be prepared in 30 minutes or less. Choose one that you are comfortable with cooking and serving.

Before the ladies arrive have the kitchen prepared for ease of demonstration. In other words lay out all the necessary utensils and ingredients. Any preparation such as chopping onions or marinating meats should be done in advance. Explain what you are doing. Do not assume that everyone knows how to cook. During this demonstration tell them some practical cooking tips. This demo can be done by you or someone that you know.

STEP THREE: 45 MINUTES—DINING AND CHAPTER 14

Discuss Ten Smart Cooking Tips in this chapter during or shortly after the meal. This is something that can be eliminated if you are short on time. You may have already incorporated some smart cooking tips during your demonstration. Remember to stay on schedule as much as possible as an act of kindness.

CURRICULUM: A SANCTUARY OF LOVE

STEP THREE: 60 MINUTES—CHAPTER 2

Move to the living room or family room. The mentor may discuss the principles found in Chapter 2, The Also Principle, or play the accompanying CD.

STEP FOUR: 15 MINUTES—DISCUSSION

If the ladies have already read Chapter 2 before attending the meeting, allow time to share from the Also Principle Study Guide.

STEP FIVE: 5 MINUTES—CLOSING

Announce the date of the next meeting. Ask them to read Chapters 3 and 8. Conclude the evening with a smile, a hug, and a word of thanks for coming. Remember the courtesy of ending on time.

SESSION 5 – RECOMMENDED FORMAT

ALLOW 3 HOURS FOR THIS SESSION

10 minutes	Greeting
60 minutes	Formal dinner style meal
A HAVEN OF PEACE	
45 minutes	Ch. 8 Priority Management
10 minutes	Discussion
A SANCTUARY OF LOVE	
45 minutes	Ch. 3 Use-What-You-Have Principle
10 minutes	Closing

STEP ONE: 10 MINUTES—GREETING

Welcome each guest enthusiastically as you greet them at the front door. Lead them to your table.

STEP TWO: 60 MINUTES—FORMAL DINNER

You may want to ask someone outside of your group to assist you with this meal preparation, serving, and clean-up. Soft lighting and background music will enhance the atmosphere. Have the table preset before guests arrive. Use whatever you have to attractively decorate your table. You can have ice water on the table and candles ready to light for this special occasion meal. The plates may be filled from the kitchen and brought to the table after all guests have been seated.

CURRICULUM: A HAVEN OF PEACE
STEP THREE: CHAPTER 12

At this meal share with them some important tips on Setting an Attractive Table and Serving from Chapter 12. Remember to never bring your book to the table to teach from unless everyone is finished and the table is partially cleared. Also, cameras, books, and other items should never be placed on the table during the meal time.

STEP FOUR: 45 MINUTES—CHAPTER 8

Move to the living room or family room. The mentor may talk about the principles found in Chapter 8, Priority Management, or play the CD accompanying this section.

STEP FIVE: 10 MINUTES—DISCUSSION

Allow for some discussion time afterward. If the ladies have already read Chapter 8 before attending the meeting, they may want to share from their Priority Management study guide.

CURRICULUM: A SANCTUARY OF LOVE
STEP SIX: 45 MINUTES—CHAPTER 3

Ask the ladies to turn to Chapter 3, Use-What-You-Have Principle. The mentor may talk about the principles found in the book or play the CD accompanying this section. You may want to add a demonstration of ways that you have used what you have. Allow for some discussion time afterward.

STEP SEVEN: 10 MINUTES—CLOSING

Announce the date of the next meeting. You may want to plan a tea party instead of a dinner for Session 6. If so, inform the ladies of this change. Remind them to read Chapters 5 and 6 on Vital Relationship Skills. Conclude the evening with a smile, a hug, and a word of thanks for coming.

SESSION 6 – RECOMMENDED FORMAT

ALLOW THREE HOURS AND 15 MINUTES FOR THIS SESSION

10 minutes	Greeting

A SANCTUARY OF LOVE

60 minutes	Ch. 5 Personality Dynamics
45 minutes	A Tea Party
45 minutes	Ch. 6 Reducing Family Conflicts
15 minutes	Discussion

A HAVEN OF PEACE

15 minutes	Ch. 13 Home Décor: Something from Nothing Decorating
5 minutes	Closing

STEP ONE: 10 MINUTES—GREETING

Welcome each guest enthusiastically as you greet them at the front door with a smile and a hug. Lead them into your living room.

CURRICULUM: A SANCTUARY OF LOVE

STEP TWO: 60 MINUTES—CHAPTER 5

In the living room or family room the mentor may talk about the Personality Dynamics found in Chapter 5 or play the CD that accompanies this section. Allow for some discussion time afterward.

STEP THREE: 45 MINUTES—TEA TIME

A tea party is a wonderful way to bring charm and beauty to those you mentor. Make it as elegant or as stylish as you like. Use whatever you have to make your table look attractive. The tea cups, small luncheon plates, serving trays, and other items do not have to match. Candles, soft lighting, and background music will enhance the atmosphere. Have the table set and everything ready before the guests arrive. You may want to ask someone who is not from the mentoring group to help you serve and clean up.

What should you serve for your tea party? A tea may include an assortment of dainty sandwiches such as: cucumber, egg, ham, and tuna salad. Scones, lemon curd, and bite-size pastries may also be served. A nontraditional tea may include freshly baked cookies, cake, or dessert. Whatever you serve, keep in mind that the best part of the tea is the warm fellowship and conversation you have with each other.

STEP FOUR: 45 MINUTES—CHAPTER 6

Ask the ladies to move to the meeting room for the presentation of Chapter 6, Reducing Family Conflicts. You may talk about this chapter of the book or play the CD that accompanies this section. Allow for some discussion time afterwards. If the ladies have already read the chapters before attending the meeting, they may want to share from their study guide.

CURRICULUM: A HAVEN OF PEACE

STEP FIVE: 15 MINUTES—CHAPTER 13

Have fun with Chapter 13, Home Décor–Something from Nothing, by creating a decorating demonstration. Put the Use-What-You-Have-Principle into practice. Your demonstration should be prepared ahead of time. Make it practical, doable, and fun!

STEP SIX: 5 MINUTES—CLOSING

Announce the date of the final meeting. This session will not include a dinner. Remind them to eat before they come. A light dessert or snack will be served. Ask them to read Chapter 15, Pass the Principles, before next session. Those ladies who desire hosting *A Home Mentoring Experience* should also read Chapters 16-18. They will need to bring their Bible along with their book to the last session. This last session will be very special and critical that the ladies attend since it will include a special time of prayer and impartation.

SESSION 7 FINAL SESSION – RECOMMENDED FORMAT

ALLOW TWO HOURS AND FORTY FIVE MINUTES FOR THIS SESSION.

This session is your final time together and is very different from your previous sessions. The purpose of this session is to hear from one another, to worship together, and to pray for one another. It will be very special to everyone who is there.

10 minutes	Greeting
A SANCTUARY OF LOVE	
30 minutes	Ch. 15 Pass the Principles
30 minutes	Dessert and beverage
A HAVEN OF PEACE	
50 minutes	The Finale
30 minutes	Prayer and impartation
10 minutes	Closing

STEP ONE: 10 MINUTES—GREETING

Welcome each guest enthusiastically as you greet them at the front door with a smile and a hug. Lead them in to your living room for your final time together.

CURRICULUM: A SANCTUARY OF LOVE
STEP TWO: 30 MINUTES—
COMMISSIONING TO PASS THE PRINCIPLES

Discuss Chapter 15, Pass the Principles, explaining the mandate to pass on what they have learned to others and to our next generation. Please read Titus 2:3-5 and discuss why this scripture passage is so important. Help the group to see that they are part of a huge revolution to transform homes everywhere. They have joined this revolution of revelation.

STEP THREE: 30 MINUTES—SERVE DESSERT AND BEVERAGE

Serve the food at the table or in the meeting room. This is a time to personally edify each other and tell your new friends how unique and special they are. Be sure you all have exchanged contact information so you can keep in touch with one another.

CURRICULUM: A HAVEN OF PEACE
STEP FOUR: 50 MINUTES—THE FINALE

The purpose of the Finale session is to send each wonderful friend home with a commission and a blessing. Commission her to pass the principles to others. Extend a prayer of blessing for her revelation to be enlarged in every aspect of her life. Details of how this can be done are given below.

This session is very special. You do not need to plan a meal unless you desire. A dessert or light snack and a beverage would be wonderful. After a time of socializing and eating, lead your guests to the living room. Furniture should be arranged in a circle where each person is visible to the other. Explain what is planned for this time so they will know what to expect and will be comfortable. Tell them that this finale session is divided into the following four parts:

- Worship with the Word
- Worship meditation
- Personal declaration
- Prayer of impartation

FIRST: WORSHIP WITH THE WORD

The purpose of this experience is to focus on the Lord by reading and meditating on specific Bible verses. Assign the following scripture passages to each group member. You will notice that these passages exalt Christ in all His majesty and power. Do not offer any remarks or teaching after the scriptures are read. Let the Bible passages speak for themselves. The verses are:

- Psalm 97:1-6
- Isaiah 6:1-4
- Ezekiel 1:22-28
- 2 Samuel 22:7-14
- Revelation 1:12-18
- Revelation 4:1-11
- Revelation 5:6-14
- Revelation 7:9-12
- Revelation 22:7, 12-16, 20-21
- Colossians 1:9-20

Allow a few minutes for them to read silently their assigned passage. The verses are to be read in the order given above. Ask them to read aloud the text without stating the reference. When one person is finished, without introduction, the next person begins. This will make the readings sound like one continuous voice. When the readings are complete, begin a quiet worship CD for the worship meditation.

SECOND: WORSHIP MEDITATION

Allow the ladies to sit relaxed in a meditative mood and listen to the words of your selected song. As they listen, give them freedom to worship in their own way. Some may want to sit, others may want to stand, kneel, raise their hands, sing, bow, or use other biblical expressions of worship.

Clearly communicate to the ladies that this is not a time to ask God for something. This is a time to exalt the Lord for who He is and what He has done in your life.

THIRD: PERSONAL DECLARATION

Background worship music can be playing softly as each lady shares what the Home Mentoring Experience has meant to her. Five to eight minutes each should be more than enough time. Watch the time carefully so every woman can share.

Focus their sharing by asking the following two questions:
1. What has this Home Mentoring Experience meant to you personally?
2. What principle or session was most impacting to you? Why?

FOURTH: PRAYER

Increase the background music volume and begin praying for one another. This allows for more privacy. Your prayer ought to include:

- Power of the Holy Spirit in her personal life to obey in all areas
- Peace of God which passes all understanding
- Courage to submit to the Word of God
- Wisdom and the love of God to permeate her life and all her relationships

Read aloud this prayer over the ladies in your group:

Thank you, Lord for the power of your Word. I pray that you, God, will
give each of my friends courage to apply every principle that they have
learned during our time together. Surround her with your love and peace;
and strengthen her to guard the love and peace in her home. Fill her with your joy
as she makes new choices every day. Bless every person that her life influences.
May she do them good and not harm all the days of her life. In Jesus' name I pray.

Amen

FINAL BLESSING FROM THE MENTOR

Speak this blessing to your ladies as you conclude. Below is an example of what you may want to include in your blessing. Be sure to pray and allow the Holy Spirit to guide you. Be sure to make eye contact with them as you read the blessing.

I commission you and bless you as you go
to be the keeper of your home. I am sending you
with a greater sense of responsibility—
a higher understanding of the value of the home
to help form the human heart.
Do not fear. Trust love—God's love through you—
to change a human heart,
both yours and those closest to you.

ENDING SCRIPTURE

"Do not be anxious about anything, but in everything,
by prayer and petition, with thanksgiving,
present your requests to God. And the peace of God,
which transcends all understanding,
will guard your hearts and your minds in Christ Jesus."

PHILIPPIANS 4:6

STEP FIVE: 10 MINUTES—FAREWELL

Lovingly bid your friends farewell. Walk them to the door and hug them goodbye. Keep in touch with them to encourage them in their new commitments to the truths and standards that were raised during this *Home Mentoring Experience.*

"Older women likewise are to be reverent in their behavior, not malicious gossips, nor enslaved to much wine, teaching what is good, that they may encourage the young women to love their husbands, to love their children, to be sensible, pure, workers at home (keepers of the home KJV), kind, being subject to their own husbands, that the word of God may not be dishonored."

Titus 2:3-5 NASB

THE HOME MENTORING REVOLUTION

INVITE THREE LADIES TO YOUR HOME

We have the potential of restoring the dignity and sanctity of our homes in America and abroad through this grass roots movement. Together we can unite and bring our families back home. Won't you join in this revolution? Here's how:

- Host a *Home Mentoring Experience*
- Mentor women in your community
- Promote godly family values
- Encourage healthy friendships

HOW YOU CAN MAKE A DIFFERENCE

Invite a minimum of three ladies to your home for a *Home Mentoring Experience.* As you share a meal or refreshment together, you will learn from each other. Together you will discuss the principles that are in THE HOME EXPERIENCE. Each lady you mentor will want to have a copy of this book.

Here are some of the wonderful benefits for both you and others who choose to host a *Home Mentoring Experience* group:

GREATER ACCOUNTABILITY You will hold yourself accountable to what you have learned while attending either a Mentoring Intensive at The Mentoring Mansion or attending a local *Home Mentoring Experience* group.

FOCUSED LIVING Preparing your home and your table for your own family members and for other guests will help you to remain focused. Remember that two to three months is long enough to break old habits and create healthy ones.

INSPIRING OTHERS   The ladies that you invite to a *Home Mentoring Experience* group will be motivated and inspired to restore their homes to greater values.

BUILDING FRIENDSHIPS   Your relationships will blossom as you work, share, and pray together. You will build confidence in those you mentor to pass on this exciting home revolution to others. These new friendships will continue to grow.

SHOWING HOSPITALITY   You will have the joy of inviting guests into your home and using what you have. Your "things" will take on a new purpose.

JOINING THE REVOLUTION   By agreeing to mentor others, you will impact many homes in addition to your own with lasting changes. You will be significant in helping to build this fast growing revolutionary movement to restore the dignity and sanctity of the home.

THE REVOLUTIONARY MULTIPLICATION OF THE HOME MENTORING EXPERIENCE

HOW IT BEGAN

Devi Titus, founder of The Mentoring Mansion was the key to birthing this revolution. In the late summer of 2002 Devi, Marilyn, and a small group of dedicated women started what became known as the *revolution of a revelation.* This revolution was birthed through prayer, hard work, and obedience. You can read more about this incredible story in the chapter entitled *The Birth of a Dream.*

THE MENTORING MANSION

The Mentoring Mansion ministry offers the comprehensive, four-day HOME Mentoring Intensives. This unique training is designed to introduce greater value into your home. While at a HOME Mentoring Intensive new creative home management techniques and vital relationship skills are introduced.

Currently eight to ten women spend four days in a luxury mansion setting with Devi and her associates. This intimate encounter inspires and equips ladies to develop an atmosphere of love, peace, and joy in their homes.

Afterward, the women are encouraged to pass on what they have learned by mentoring a minimum of three women. The data of this multiplication process is given later in this chapter.

TRAINING FOR RAPID GROUP MULTIPLICATION

HOW CAN I GET THIS STARTED IN MY LOCAL CHURCH? The Mentoring Mansion ministry sends out Mansion Mentors to launch the *Home Mentoring Experience* in churches. The Mansion Mentor along with her assistant will conduct an abbreviated Home Mentoring Intensive with local church leaders and selected women. Ideally the time frame for this launch begins on Friday at 5:00 pm and concludes on Saturday at 5:00 pm. This focused training will be for those who desire to host or assist a *Home Mentoring Experience* following the completion of the Launch.

STARTING A HOME MENTORING EXPERIENCE GROUP After the Home Experience Launch training sessions these ladies will be ready to begin *Home Mentoring Experience* groups. Remember that these groups must always meet in a home setting. In this way, multiplication begins right away.

Just think, this mentoring revolution model has the potential of bringing all church ladies to someone's table to learn creative home management and vital relationships skills.

REVOLUTIONARY IMPACT

You have the potential of reaching your community, building relationships, and impacting vast numbers of families. Let me explain to you how the multiplication works. You will meet with a minimum of three women in your home once a week or every other week for seven sessions. I chose the number three because even a small studio apartment has space for you and three more. However, I encourage you to invite the number of ladies who can be seated at your table. Hopefully, you will inspire those three or more women to meet with three more women. In this way the *Home Mentoring Experience* multiplies every three months. Imagine, just the first ten participants carry the potential to reach over 143 million women after only three years!

Here is an example showing how just ten women can carry a message that will reach millions worldwide. Together we will lead a Home Revolution of Revelation that HOME is a place of love and peace.

FIRST YEAR MULTIPLICATION The Mentoring Mansion equips ten women to restore love and peace in their homes and to mentor other women to do the same.

- Each of those 10 train 3 women = 30 women impacted
- Each of those 30 trains 3 = 90
- Each of those 90 trains 3 = 270
- Each of those 270 trains 3 = 810
- Each of those 810 trains 3 = **2,430**

SECOND YEAR MULTIPLICATION

- Each of those 2430 trains 3 = 7290
- Each of those 7,290 trains 3 = 21,870
- Each of those 21,870 trains 3 = 65,610
- Each of those 65,610 trains 3 = 196,830
- Each of those 196,830 trains 3 = **590,490**

THIRD YEAR MULTIPLICATION

- Each of those 590,490 trains 3 = 1,771,470
- Each of those 1,771,470 trains 3 = 5,314,410
- Each of those 5,314,410 trains 3 = 15, 943,230
- Each of those 15,943,230 trains 3 = 47,829,690
- Each of those 47,829,690 trains 3 = **143,489,070** women impacted

If only one percent of women actually follow through, we can still expect to reach over one million women from our first group of ten. Keep in mind, the Mentoring Mansion mentors a new group of ten women each month. This potential is huge!

* These calculations are conservative considering only five revolutions per year. I have only calculated meetings being conducted for 35 weeks out of 52 per year, allowing for down time between each mentoring group. You can agree that we can make an impact.

YOU CAN MAKE A DIFFERENCE! Won't you join in our revolution of revelation?

PLEASE NOTIFY US

When you begin to host a *Home Mentoring Experience* in your home, please notify us so we can track the impact of this Home Mentoring Revolution to restore families. Together, we can transform family statistics!

We want to know your name and the names of your mentees. Please register on our website and click on the Mentoring Revolution.

Additional copies of THE HOME EXPERIENCE can be ordered from the web site.

www.mentoringmansion.com

"Therefore everyone who hears these words of mine and puts them into practice is like a wise man who built his house on the rock. The rain came down, the streams rose, and the winds blew and beat against that house; yet it did not fall, because it had its foundation on the rock."

~ Matthew 7: 24-25

"So now I charge you... commands of the LORD possess this good land tance to your descenda

Be careful to follow all the your God, that you may and pass it on as an inheri- nts forever."

— 1 Chronicles 28:8

P.

THE MENTORING MANSION STORY— THE BIRTH OF DEVI'S DREAM

My husband, Larry, and I had completed forty years of full-time pastoral ministry when we decided to retire. Although I had a fulfilling ministry at the time, speaking around the country to sometimes 20,000 women a year, the decision still terrified me. After four successful pastorates with my husband, I could not imagine life outside the local church—my first love—and not mentoring women from this venue.

During over forty years of marriage and pastoral ministry, we also nurtured more than eighty young people who lived in our home at one time or another, many of whom are now in full-time ministry. Though my primary role was to support my husband and joyfully raise our two incredible children, our home was open to relational discipleship. Mentoring was like second nature. It reached the printed page when I launched the first Christian women's magazine *VIRTUE*, elevating the biblical mandate for women in the height of feminism.

I had hoped some day to open a development center that would train women in creative home management and vital relationship skills necessary in our changing society. I periodically looked for a location to fulfill my dream. Often I asked the Lord, "Is it here? Is it now?" But I heard nothing. When we moved to Youngstown, Ohio, in 1995 to plant what would be our final church to pastor, it seemed as if the dream had died.

THE CONCEPTION OF MY DREAM

As this new season of life began to take hold, I thought more about mentoring from my home. Then three months before leaving our pastorate, Larry was hospitalized with genetic heart problems and open-heart surgery was scheduled in August 2001. I was again faced with uncertainty.

At the same time a historical home built in 1915 across the street listed for sale. Larry toured the home while I was on a speaking trip and called me immediately. He excitedly told me that he was sure I would want to sell our home and buy this one, which was twice as large as ours. Surprisingly, I did not want to live in this 8,000 square foot historic home.

Although I did not want to buy the "mansion," on my way home from the hospital one day I saw someone in the driveway looking at this magnificent home. I spontaneously spoke out within my car, "Get out of my driveway!"

Later while praying, distraught over Larry's condition, I concluded my prayer, "And by the way, Lord, why do I not want to live in that house but do not want any one else to buy it?" Clearly, the Lord answered, *"Twenty years ago, I gave you a dream to mentor women in creative home management and vital relationship skills. That is not your home. That is your dream-come-true. It is your "Mentoring Mansion."*

ENLARGING OF THE DREAM—THE SONOGRAM

My pursuit of purchasing this historical mansion began. Though Larry and I were in complete agreement, we were met with tremendous obstacles as we entered the process of purchasing this home. We continued to pray as I heard the continual voice of the Spirit say, *"Keep asking, keep knocking, keep seeking."* Some doors would close and others would open just enough to keep our vision alive.

During this time God began pouring revelation into my heart for The Mentoring Mansion concept. I couldn't sleep. I couldn't eat. I couldn't shop! Like a converging force I could see its purpose—the plan was very clear. This would be a center where Christian women's mindsets invaded by feminism would be restored to the plum line of biblical truth, as we conducted four-day Home Mentoring Intensives. I began building the necessary team.

I asked Marilyn Weiher to become my teaching partner. She also had a passionate dream to mentor women in a home setting. Marilyn partnered with me to write our first publication entitled The Home Mentoring Manual. Inspired by the Holy Spirit, we published this extensive manual in three months. During this time I still had no way to purchase the property. Somehow I knew that the resources were somewhere…I just had to find them.

Matthew 7:7, *"Ask, and it will be given to you; seek and you will find; knock, and it will be opened to you,"* was like a pulse in my spirit, day and night, rejection after rejection. The pressing resistance was only equaled by the weight of a ringing promise: Keep asking. Keep seeking. Keep knocking. For months this was my only source of hope.

Then in January 2002, we finally took the leap of faith and made the official offer to purchase the mansion, but at $100,000 less than the original asking price. I went further than that, I also *asked* the owners to donate all of the furnishings and antiques that were in the home. Incredibly, the owner said, "Yes!"

BIRTHING PAINS

But there is no birth without pain. Just prior to full delivery of a baby, when the head crowns, the life of that baby is at its greatest risk. It is now that the bearing down pain comes, the focus—the push that brings life. The pain is indescribable but nothing else in life matters until that mother hears the cry of her baby. So it was with birthing our dream.

Our offer to purchase the Mansion was miraculously accepted, but it was contingent on the sale of another parcel of real estate. In four months we had a buyer and the process was in motion. Although the official sale was not closed, the banker assured us that we had a guaranteed loan from our purchaser.

Based on that, by faith, we printed brochures and launched the promotion of The Mentoring Mansion, just in time for the 2002 International Foursquare convention being held at Denver, CO in April where more than 3,000 delegates would hear about this new national ministry.

The day before flying out, however, I received a call from our daughter. Her husband had filed for divorce. As much as I wanted to be with her, I was trapped; I was to speak in Las Vegas and then open the Mansion's exhibit at the convention in Colorado. I had to trust.

Two days later while in Las Vegas, I received another call. It was my daddy, informing me that Mother was dying in the hospital in California. My heart was heavy as I headed to Colorado. While I set up the exhibit booth, enthusiastically branding conventioneers with glimmering gold "Mentoring Mansion" stickers, my cell phone rang. It was the banker informing me that they had withdrawn the previously approved loan of our buyers. This now prevented us from closing on the purchase of the mansion.

It seemed like my world crashed. I was promoting something that didn't exist. Filled with emotional pain and discouragement, I heard the Spirit softly say, "Keep asking. Keep knocking. Keep seeking."

THE BIRTH

The next three months were the most horrible months of my life. I worked on the renovations to the exterior of the mansion just as though everything was on schedule. As I scraped off the old chipped paint and repainted the ninety-three windows in the home, I prayed, "I will not be bitter or resentful if I do not get this home. I will do this as a labor of love to the owners. But please, O God, give me a miracle way to buy this home." My mustard seed of faith was accompanied by months of hard work, day and night, in the midst of my daughter's crisis and my mother's serious illness.

With August just around the corner and ladies registering for the first Home Mentoring Intensive to open August 1st, reality set in. We still had no money to buy the mansion. In my deep despair, I awakened at five o'clock dreading daylight, knowing that I would make the decision to no longer pursue the purchase of the Mansion. Every door seemed closed. I cried. I prayed—and then, I heard an inner voice that said, "First Chronicles."

I opened my Bible to I Chronicles 28:20: *"Be strong and courageous, and do the work. Do not be afraid or discouraged, for the Lord God is with you. He will not fail you or forsake you until all the work, for the service of the house of the Lord is finished. ...and every willing man skilled in any craft will help you in all the work."*

This scripture was so specific that it gave me hope to continue in faith as we attempted to sell our property and prepare the exterior of the mansion for our hopeful grand opening August 1st.

Only ten days before the opening, the answer came, the purchase was made and we got the key! Forty skilled craftsmen came locally and from across the country to assist us. The entire home was readied to receive our first guests.

On August 1, 2002 the first Home Mentoring Intensive was conducted as scheduled. It was like the cry of a mother's baby.

My mother's health is well. My daughter's marriage is restored. Six hundred women came to our first Mentoring Mansion in Youngstown, OH in the first three years. Monthly women continue to spend four days at the new Dallas/Ft.Worth, TX mansion. Now countless women are making their homes havens of peace and sanctuaries of love. When our mentees return home, many of them are hosting *The Home Mentoring Experience,* where a small group of friends meet together to pass on the impacting principles they learned from The Mentoring Mansion and THE HOME EXPERIENCE book. Truly a revolution of revelation has begun. For current information on our Dallas/Ft.Worth Metroplex Mentoring Mansion site and an update on this rapid growing revolution visit our web site.

RESOURCE CENTER

WWW.MENTORINGMANSION.COM

ORDERING FROM THE WEB
- *THE HOME EXPERIENCE* book
- *THE DINNER EXPERIENCE* by Devi Titus

ACCOMPANING CDs and DVDs BY:
Devi Titus
- The Dignity and Sanctity of the Home.
- The Also Principle
- The Use- What- You- Have Principle
- The Table Principle

Marilyn Weiher
- Personality Dynamics
- Reducing Family Conflicts
- Honoring Your Husband
- Priority Management

OTHER LIFE TRANSFORMING MESSAGES ON CD
Our resources provide life transforming messages that strengthen men and women to make wiser choices.

INFORMATION ON THE WEB
The Mentoring Mansion—Home Mentoring Intensives

Attend a four-day luxury Home Mentoring Intensive with Devi and Marilyn at The Mentoring Mansion.

Home Mentoring Experience Groups

Launch a Home Mentoring Experience Group in your local church or community. Become part of a national and global movement to restore the dignity and sanctity of the home.

To Schedule Speaking Engagements

Devi Titus speaks at conferences, seminars, and retreats. Her years of ministry have life transforming impact.

Marilyn Weiher speaks at women's ministry events. She is a Mentoring Mansion Mentor and launches Home Mentoring Experience Groups in local churches.

1